Gerry Faust

Gerry Faust

Notre Dame's Man in Motion

From Moeller High
to Notre Dame

Denny Dressman

SAN DIEGO • NEW YORK
A. S. BARNES & COMPANY, INC.
IN LONDON:
THE TANTIVY PRESS

First Edition
Manufactured in the United States of America

For information write to:
A.S. Barnes & Company, Inc.
P.O. Box 3051
La Jolla, California 92038

The Tantivy Press
Magdalen House
136-148 Tooley Street
London, SE1 2TT, England

Library of Congress Cataloging in Publication Data

Dressman, Denny.
   Gerry Faust: from Moeller High to Notre Dame.

   1. Faust, Gerry. 2. Football coaches — United States —
Biography. 3. Moeller High School — Football. 4. University of
Notre Dame. I. Title.
GV939.F28D73   796.332′092′4 [B]   81-3592
ISBN 0-498-02573-X   AACR2

1 2 3 4 5 6 7 8 9 84 83 82 81

The heights by great men reached and kept
Were not attained by sudden flight,
But they, while their companion slept,
Were toiling upward in the night.

—Henry Wadsworth Longfellow
The Ladder of St. Augustine

Much of this book was written late at night, very late. It is dedicated to the woman who often fell asleep on the floor of my office at home, Melanie, my wife and inspiration, and to our daughter and our joy, Melissa, who slept in the room overhead, her dreams punctuated by the muffled pounding of her father's typewriter.

Cincinnati, 1981   D. D.

This book is dedicated, also, to my wife, Marlene, and our children, Julie Marie, Gerry, and Steve, and my mother-in-law, Angela, for their understanding and love through so many nights when I was away from home; to my parents, Fuzzy and Alma, an inspiration as well as an example during my growing years; to my sister, Marilee, her husband Ken, and my brother Fred for their support; and to all my friends in coaching and teaching, for their kindness and help.

South Bend, 1981   G. F.

Contents

Acknowledgments

I wish to thank my good friend, Jim Delaney, for his valuable counsel and sincere interest in this project; Father Lawrence Krusling and the faculty and coaches at Moeller High School for their warm hospitality and generous cooperation; Michael Keating and Ed Reinke, outstanding photographers, for jobs well done; the Faust family; *The Cincinnati Enquirer,* for permission to write this book while remaining a member of the news staff; and, most of all, my wife Melanie, who urged me to try it and read every line three times.

Special appreciation, also, to my editor, Ellen Bevier Turner; only I can see her fine touch in the refinement of my work.

Moeller High School photo.

Prologue

As the Cessna 310 dropped out of the clouds at about 3,000 feet our pilot, Don Turner, pointed to his right. There in the distance, barely visible, was the Golden Dome. It was almost 10:30. We would be on the ground at South Bend, Indiana, Airport in a matter of minutes. The press conference called to introduce Gerry Faust as Notre Dame's new head football coach was scheduled for 11 o'clock. Flying with me were my wife, Melanie, and our daughter, Melissa. They had been with me every step of the way, had followed Moeller High School on the road, had cheered every victory. Gerry Faust's moment was as much theirs as it was mine to share and savor.

"We're going to have to hurry," Melanie fretted as we taxied toward the terminal.

Press conferences can be pretty routine. Sportswriters rarely ask their best questions in open court; they are notoriously protective of their best angles. But this session figured to be different. Gerry Faust, a high school coach from Cincinnati, Ohio, had just made mankind's great leap—from Moeller High School, his home for 21 years, to the Fighting Irish of Notre Dame, America's national university.

In South Bend that morning, one radio announcer had called him "Gary Frost." Weeks earlier, on national television, Jimmy the Greek had said, "Gerry Who? Never heard of him," when asked for odds on the one rumor considered hardly worth a serious bet.

1

Gerry's name had been mentioned for months in his hometown, but even Notre Dame sports information director Roger Valdiserri scoffed at the suggestion early that fall. "We're not running a kindergarten program," he told a Cincinnati writer, declaring the Faust possibility an impossibility. This press conference was going to be fun.

Our cab driver pretended not to know what was going on at the university. "A new coach? Who got it, Lou Holtz? Joe Restic? Don Shula?" All of those battle-tested, household names had been rumored for the Notre Dame job at one time or other. So had several others. We played along with the cabbie.

"Some *High School* coach!!" The driver feigned shock. "Better say a prayer for that guy. Wait till he loses a game. Wait till he starts hearing from the alumni. I wouldn't want *that* job." We rolled up to the Athletic and Convocation Center at two minutes before 11. As we got out of the cab, Gerry was strolling toward us with Father Edmund Joyce.

"Denny!!" I went up to Gerry and congratulated him. He looked uncharacteristically nervous. His mouth was drawn, and he seemed uncomfortable. Maybe he was in awe. Maybe he was exhausted. Maybe it was just the blue pin-striped suit, soft blue dress shirt, and brand new shoes. He did not look at all like the Gerry Faust I knew. Underneath that dressy exterior there has to be a Moeller T-shirt, I thought.

I had been with Gerry the previous afternoon, only hours before the announcement cleared the Associated Press wire. "I haven't gotten a call yet," he had said. "But if I do, I'm going to hit the road. I'm going to be unavailable to all the media until a press conference. That gives everybody an equal shot.

"Don't worry," he assured me, "you'll have time to get up to South Bend if it happens."

Gerry was now introducing me to Father Joyce, the man who picked him for the job. Father Joyce is a powerful man whose strong personality controls the Notre Dame athletic department.

"Denny's one of my best friends," Gerry said, seeming to relax a little. "He's writing a book about me. He's been following me everywhere for months."

Father Joyce greeted me pleasantly, but kept Gerry moving toward the great arena where Notre Dame's rich athletic tradition is on display for all to see.

"You need a ride back to Cincinnati?" Gerry invited. "You can go back with Marlene and me. We're driving back tonight."

Gerry spotted Don Turner in the lobby and was genuinely surprised. "What are *you* doing here!" Don explained that he was our pilot. Don had transported Gerry and other Moeller coaches on several scouting trips during the season. "You know that time you flew me to Indianapolis for a speech?" Gerry confided with a grin. "I met Father Joyce about this job."

The podium was elevated. Behind it was a blue banner 40 or 50 feet long that proclaimed, "The Fighting Irish." Seated on the platform with Gerry were Father Joyce; Gerry's predecessor Dan Devine; retiring athletic director (AD) Moose Krause, the department's last link with Knute Rockne; and incoming AD Gene Corrigan.

Among the hundred or so sportswriters, photographers, sportscasters, and camera crews in the audience was Bill Gleason of the Chicago *Sun-Times,* who had published an exclusive story naming Gerry the new Irish coach 38 days before it was official. Joe Doyle of the South Bend *Tribune,* was there, too. Doyle had likened the speculation to a horse race and, under the headline "The Irish Sweepstakes," had made Gerry a 50-to-1 longshot. Also in attendance were Dave Diles of ABC, who would be favored with a separate taping session because of the network's exclusive coverage of NCAA football, and the Ohio contingent—three TV crews, one radio sports director, three reporters and two photographers from Cincinnati, three teams from Gerry's hometown of Dayton, and the Irish wit of Ohio sportswriting, Danny Coughlin of the Cleveland *Plain Dealer.*

Gerry spotted my wife and daughter in the audience as he accepted the place behind the microphones from Father Joyce. He gestured and silently formed the words, "Hi, Mel." He was honored that she was present.

His first words to the press were great copy. Gerry talked of dreaming about this day, about singing the Notre Dame fight song while riding his bike to and from CYO football practice in the fifth grade. He explained that his tie, a dark blue one with pale shamrocks—Notre Dame Fighting Irish shamrocks—was a gift from a Denver businessman. He had told the man he would wear it only if he ever got the Notre Dame coaching job. And, he said Notre Dame was the only place that could tear him away from his beloved Moeller High.

"The toughest thing I've ever done was leaving Moeller yesterday," he said. "It's very difficult after twenty-one years to leave some place you love."

I sat taking notes, and thought about what my family and I were seeing. We had returned to our hometown, Cincinnati, in 1969 so I could be a sportswriter for *The Enquirer.* I started on preps, and my first stories were preseason previews. I had asked Gerry about his team's weaknesses. Most coaches would have given a general answer—offense or defense, depth or size, or speed or experience. Moeller's weakness that year, Gerry concluded after some serious head-scratching, was defensive ends. This is not an ordinary high school team, I thought. Moeller overcame its deficiencies that year to win all 10 games. I watched and wrote about Gerry and Moeller for seven seasons. I saw him win, and I saw him lose: an unforgettable 6–3 upset in a freak snowstorm in early November 1971 that ruined a perfect season; a humbling 34–7 rout the first time Moeller qualified for the state playoffs; and another playoff defeat the next year.

We shared a few social evenings, too, including one memorable visit to my home. When I broke out a jigsaw puzzle of a *Playboy* centerfold, Gerry, a very religious man, was embarassed. He did not decline to work on the puzzle, he merely blushed and tried to force a few jokes until we finished. He still talks about it, shaking his head with an "I don't believe it" smile.

I moved from the sports department to the news department after Moeller's first state championship in 1975 and watched from a distance as Gerry's empire grew. After four more state championships, three national championships, and talk of an international game in Japan, I called him in May 1980.

"I think there's a book in you and the Moeller football program," I said. "There isn't anything like it."

Gerry had turned down other proposals because he did not know the people who would be involved.

"If you're going to write it yourself," he said, "I'll do it." It was then that he told me the book might have another angle.

"I think I might have a shot at the Notre Dame job if it opens up," he said. Six months later I found myself on the Notre Dame campus, watching it all come true.

There were 43 questions asked before Father Joyce called a halt and turned Gerry over to the TV crews. The press asked about his theories of coaching, inquired about the status of the current

Notre Dame staff and his plans for naming new assistants, and quizzed him at length on the challenges he would face moving from high school to college. There was a distinct tone of doubt to these questions:

"Will you have to change your philosophy or approach at college?"

"What makes you believe you're ready at this time in your life to move from high school to college coaching?"

"Have you given *any thought* to the pressures at Notre Dame?"

"Do you think 18- or 19-year-olds will be as open to your learning process as the children you've been working with?"

"Because of Notre Dame's tradition, is it easier to start a college coaching career at Notre Dame than at another college?"

Gerry answered with sincerity. He said the biggest adjustment would be "learning how things work around here." He said he would have to change some things in his approach, of course, "but, I'm not going to change myself." He knew he was ready for college men, he answered, because he had addressed minor league baseball players and major league businessmen, and both groups were ready to play for him. "There is always a lot of pressure with our winning streaks," he said. Gerry just did not expect to have a problem getting Notre Dame players to perform for him.

"Did you get a raise?" Dan Coughlin piped up.

Someone asked Father Joyce about the selection process, noting that Moeller had sent more players to Notre Dame than any other school (14 in the 1970s). "Did that cause you to look to him?"

Father Joyce had tipped his hand a couple of years earlier at a banquet in Cincinnati. "We owe him a lot," he had said then. "He has sent us many fine young men. He is the kind of man we want our coaches to be." Now, in response to the question, Father Joyce said, "Yes. We were very impressed and very pleased. Very few of the Moeller boys have gone to the pros; they've just been the kind of student-athletes Notre Dame wants." Asked how many candidates were interviewed, Joyce responded, "Not very many. We did a lot of internal screening. We are well aware of the candidates."

The questioners returned to Gerry, and the skeptical press did its best to test him.

"Doesn't being a high school coach with a limited frame of reference hamper you in recruiting?"

Gerry had the perfect reply. "Not really. We've played Pittsburgh Penn Hills, DeMatha from Maryland, Dallas Jesuit; next year we play Bethel from Virginia and Servite from California. I know the football played around the country. We've had a recruiter from practically every school in the country visit Moeller in the last few years. I know who the good ones are."

Gerry has always enjoyed the press. His attitude is a rarity. "You have a job to do and I have a job to do," he has said to hundreds of reporters. "I'll always be honest with you, and I'll cooperate in every way I can as long as you don't burn me." After the thirty-first question, Gerry spoke his piece to the assembled Notre Dame press corps. "If I can ever help you out in any way," he began, "I hope you'll ask. I know you've got a job to do, and I hope we have a great relationship."

Bill Gleason jumped on the opening. "To help us, then, give us your local phone number."

The next question was personal. "Do you have a cold, or is your voice always like that?" Gerry was fine; he has sounded like the late actor Andy Devine for most of his adult life.

Dan Coughlin asked the last two questions. "Did what you made as a motivational speaker equal what you made at Moeller?" Yes. "Combined, are you still getting a pay raise here?"

Half an hour after the press conference ended, Gerry had not made it beyond the bottom of the steps leading from the podium. Between TV and radio tapings, he looked for his wife and called out, "You doing all right, Marlene?" He was on his tenth interview, she on her fifteenth.

"I'm fine," she answered.

"How many bedrooms do you need, Marlene?" her current interviewer inquired.

Gerry moved through the crowd with the confidence of a politician, but this was no act. He was being himself.

Gleason introduced himself, and Gerry noted, "I said you were sticking your neck out writing that story, but I guess you knew more than I did." Gerry laughed. "Sure glad you were right."

Joe Doyle popped up. "Fifty-to-one," Gerry kidded. "I thought that was a great article. You're a great writer."

Danny Coughlin approached and introduced himself, and Gerry blurted: "I thought I knew you when you were asking all those questions! You're getting married Saturday, aren't you? Congratulations!" A writer from Cleveland had mentioned the wedding a couple of weeks earlier. The red-faced Irishman was momentarily speechless.

The overriding theme of the day's questioning had been: "Can a virtually unknown high school coach from Cincinnati make good in the big-time college football world of small town South Bend, Indiana?" Danny Coughlin and I discussed it briefly.

"I think he'll be the greatest coach, the biggest success, and the most dynamic personality at Notre Dame since Rockne," I said.

Danny rubbed his chin. "Can I quote you on that?"

I was sure, because I knew Gerry Faust. I knew what he had done, and I knew what he could do. His story is too good to be true, but it is. Fiction like this would be ridiculed.

As our plane gained altitude heading for home, Melanie looked back at the Notre Dame campus.

"Look!" she said. "The sun has broken through the clouds right over the Golden Dome! See it shining!"

Surely it was an omen.

1

The Aura and Era of Gerry Faust

The sign in front of the school read: "Football Tickets On Sale August 4." It was the middle of July, and school would not start until August 27. This had to be Moeller High School.

The trophy case in the main lobby offered confirmation: frozen in action atop handsome walnut bases, gleaming miniature football players elbowed for recognition of their particular city, state, and national championships. Further proof was on display in the coaches' office downstairs. On the first desk inside the door: statues of the Blessed Virgin Mary and St. Jude, plus a briefcase jammed so full it could not come within five inches of closing. On the wall above the desk: a Crucifix, a few holy cards, and a collage of photos— mom, dad, wife and children, former players, and the coach himself. This was Gerry Faust's workbench, and these were reminders of those things which matter most to him.

Gerry is, all at once, all of the time, a devoted son, true friend, thoughtful husband, concerned father, and an uncommonly devout Catholic. He is not afraid to hug his father, kiss his mother, and tell them "I love you" wherever they might meet; he sends his wife thank-you notes for all she does; and he never forgets to write to his friends on every occasion of personal importance to them. Always his cards and letters are inscribed "JMJ" for Jesus, Mary, and Joseph, a carryover from his grade school days; always they end with "God Bless You." Gerry begins every day with early morning Mass wherever he is—and did so even while honeymooning in

Miami Beach. And he spends every day of the year thinking football, even during the annual family vacation. His world is a hundred yards long, with a goal post at one end and an altar at the other.

Bad knees cause Gerry to slouch, so that he looks shorter than six feet one. He does not walk; he pads along like a five-year-old in a sleeper that is too big. He embraces too vigorously; his pat on the back is too hard. He is perpetually hoarse and eternally unpretentious in his appearance. A "Coach Faust" caricature would feature rumpled hair, baggy bermuda shorts, a faded T-shirt, limp white socks sagging to the ankles, and soiled tennis shoes. He was 45 going on 12 when he left Moeller in 1980, a man permanently blessed with a boy's energy and enthusiasm. Like any seventh grader, he could live happily on vegetable soup, bologna sandwiches, and Coke; in fact, he had his own Coca-Cola tap installed in the coaches' office at Moeller. His favorite words are "first-class," "a-hundred-and-twenty-percent," "thanks a million," and "Hail Mary."

Gerry wore many hats at Moeller, none of them a teacher's in later years. He was athletic director, chief fund-raiser, program advertising sales coordinator, eighth grade student orientation director, boosters club moderator, promoter, and public relations man. He stopped teaching after Moeller's second state championship, when the demands on his time required the installation of a telephone in his classroom and caused him to miss as many typing classes as he taught.

As athletic director he was accountable for scheduling and the excellence or mediocrity of 10 other sports programs besides football. His major fund-raising effort was the financing of a million-dollar athletics, activities, and classroom building on the Moeller campus. Advertising revenues from Moeller's 200-page football program averaged $30,000 a year; the sales drive consumed six months. While enrollment at other Catholic high schools in the Cincinnati archdiocese dropped, Moeller held steady at just under a thousand boys, largely because Gerry visited every grade school assigned to Moeller and recruited the eighth grade students with a one-hour slide show and sales pitch about Moeller High. More than 500 strong, the Moeller boosters met weekly during the football season and monthly the rest of the year, supporting Gerry in countless ways.

His work as head football coach did not end with the final game. To insure his players' futures, he met with or called dozens of college coaches every week for three months and counseled the heavily recruited stars of each year's team. He also made sure that every boy who was not recruited but wanted to play football in college received the best opportunity Gerry could arrange. In his spare time he became a motivational speaker of national acclaim and traveled more than a hundred thousand miles a year to speak to business audiences.

Gerry ceased to be a high school football coach years before he left Moeller for Notre Dame, just as his program ceased to be a high school program years earlier. To most people high school football is small time, local. It is neighborhood rivals on a dimly lighted field with bleachers on one side and maybe a thousand people in the stands—all relatives, classmates, or friends of the players, coaches, and kids in the band. It is the best athletes playing both offense and defense, a final score that matters only around home, and an undefeated season once in a decade when fate combines the right sophomores, juniors, and seniors. It is a coach who teaches history or driver training or P.E., a man whose dream is *one* great player, *one* great team, and maybe one big break, like an assistant's job in college.

At Moeller, Gerry's idea of high school football was taking on champions from New York to Dallas, from Pittsburgh to Detroit— and thumping all of them. It was outdrawing the Cincinnati Reds, head to head, one Friday night, and it was being invited to play a game in Japan. It was 15 minutes on CBS and an hour with *Donahue,* a page in *TIME,* five pages in *LIFE,* a piece in the *Wall Street Journal,* and feature stories in newspapers coast-to-coast. It was 18 coaches, 24 team doctors, 210 players, and a hundred-thousand-dollar budget. In 18 varsity seasons it was 22 high school All-Americans and almost 300 college scholarships. And it was winning: 174 victories, 17 defeats, and 2 ties . . . one loss in 71 games from 1975 through 1980, five state championships, and four mythical national titles.

It was Gerry's style at Moeller to handle every detail, take every phone call, and greet every visitor. Outsiders would watch him and wonder: "Can this guy be real?" He definitely had flair. He was, in a word, colorful. Everyone who knows him has a favorite story.

The coaches and players on Moeller's first state championship team remember the night of the title game played in snowy, windy Akron, Ohio. The team left the hotel later than planned, and when the bus was stopped by a train at a railroad crossing, it seemed possible that Moeller might actually miss the kickoff. They sat, and sat, and sat; a line of cars formed behind them.

"Wait here," Gerry said to the driver.

Before anyone could say, "Where's he going?" Gerry was out of the bus and trudging down the tracks into the darkness, hunched over more than usual to shield himself from the cold. Wearing a floppy hat of alternating blue and gold panels, he looked a little bit like one of the seven dwarfs.

He returned in 10 minutes and announced triumphantly, "It's all been taken care of." Moments later a railroader slipped between two boxcars, and as though it were the Red Sea, the train parted. Moeller was on its way.

Amazed employees in the Delta Air Lines terminal at Atlanta International Airport and a planeload of still-puzzled passengers can tell about the time Gerry stopped the takeoff of a Boeing 707. He was returning from a speaking engagement and his connecting flight had arrived late.

Arriving breathless at the ticket counter, he gasped: "I'm going to Cincinnati; has my plane left yet?"

"It hasn't taken off, but it's taxiing out to the runway," the agent said apologetically. "I'm afraid you're too late."

It was a ground-level gate, and Gerry's plane was still in view, backing away from the building.

"Is *that* my plane? I gotta catch it," Gerry declared. He was out the door and running across the tarmac, waving his arms wildly, before the ticket agent could react. The pilot saw him and brought the jet back to the terminal. When Gerry boarded a few minutes later, the captain was waiting for him at the door.

"You're Gerry Faust, aren't you? We couldn't leave you behind."

Gerry took a lot of kidding from the passengers. Naturally he made the most of the situation. Seated next to him was an advertising executive for Wendy's Old Fashioned Hamburgers. Gerry had been trying unsuccessfully for months to sell Wendy's a program ad. By the time the flight arrived in Cincinnati, page 22 of the Moeller football program had been reserved for Wendy's "Crusader of the Week" salute—five free hamburgers to each lucky fan holding a program autographed by the "Crusader of the Week."

There really was no slow time of the year for Gerry; any day was like every day. Summer should have been quieter, but he needed that season to prepare for the next one. He would arrive a little after 7 each summer morning, coming to school straight from 6:30 Mass at the church next door. Until 9 o'clock most days he was alone in the cramped office that 30 members of the athletic department shared. He used the early morning to tend to the dozens of little details he would never think of leaving to chance or entrusting to anyone else. There were practice schedules to be drawn, playbooks to be assembled, locker room signs to be made, a boosters club corn roast to plan. . . . Physical exam day was drawing closer; doctors and nurses had to be called, and the chaos of that hectic morning organized as well as it could be. And tickets would be going on sale soon, as the sign out front indicated. White-haired Mr. "Bachi," the father of assistant coach Ted Bacigalupo and Moeller's ticket manager in his retirement, would sit behind a card table in front of the trophy case for eight hours a day and sell more than 10,000 tickets before the first day of classes.

The pace of each day was set by two turquoise and yellow telephones on Gerry's cluttered desk. They were the wrong shades of blue and gold, but that was as close as Cincinnati Bell could come to Moeller's colors. Starting at 9 o'clock, they rang incessantly with the essence of Gerry's existence.

"Helll-oh." The greeting rolled off worn vocal chords, ending an octave higher than it began. The first call of the day was from CINCINNATI Magazine; finishing touches on a soon-to-be-published spread about the Moeller steamroller.

"Helll-oh." On the other phone was the manager of Ohio's North-South All-Star Game; why aren't Moeller's stars interested in playing this year?

"Helll-oh." Back to the first phone, a coach from Vanderbilt; he is told, "No coach, don't come up yet. Practice doesn't start for three more weeks."

"Helll-oh." The president of a manufacturing firm was calling back weeks after trying to talk Gerry into lowering his speaking fee; yes, Gerry will speak to his sales force—for his standard $1,500 fee—if the date the man wants is still available.

"Helll-oh." It was the father of a player; he heard this song on the radio driving back from a business trip and thought it would be perfect as the coming season's pep rally theme. "That's one of the most important calls I'll get all summer," Gerry said.

The phones fell silent, as if on cue, when a tall man, graying at the temples but suntanned and looking fit, ambled into the office. Hank Bullough, recently named defensive coordinator of the Cincinnati Bengals, had a matter to discuss before leaving for training camp. The family would not be moving down from Massachusetts until a few days after the start of summer practice at Moeller. His son Shane, a six-foot-one, 195-pound *sophomore*, might miss a few days of practice.

"Don't worry, coach," Gerry said. "He can move in with us for a few days. Or if he doesn't like that idea, I'm sure one of the kids would love to have him stay until you get your family settled. It would be better than missing any practice."

Bullough left, satisfied, and as if he tripped a switch on the way out, the phones came back to life. First on the line was Cliff Stewart, a junior high football player from Lancaster, Pennsylvania.

"Yes, this is Moeller High School. This is Gerry Faust. Oh! Pleased to hear from you, Cliff. Where are you calling from? Pennsylvania! Well, I think we're going to be pretty good again this year. We're going to be kinda young. Yes. Yes. That's right, three preseason All-Americans: our fullback, Mark Brooks; Doug Williams, a tackle; and Mike Larkin, a linebacker. You know all about 'em? You must be a real Moeller fan, Cliff. Do you play football? Give me your name and address, Cliff. I'll send you a stat book and a Moeller football T-shirt. Great talking to you, Cliff! Thanks a million for calling."

Gerry was sealing the large brown envelope containing the shirt and press book when he ended the call. "I get calls like that several times a year," he said "You wouldn't believe how many people around the country follow Moeller."

From Philadelphia, a Notre Dame fan named Jim Kennedy has followed Moeller by telephone for years and become one of Gerry's closest friends. Jim is Gerry's age but was not blessed with Gerry's good health; a respiratory illness has confined him to his home since the age of 19. He began calling Moeller after Steve Sylvester and Steve Niehaus showed up at Notre Dame in the early 1970s. He wanted to know more about this school that was producing such outstanding players for his beloved Fighting Irish.

Gerry and Jim quickly found they had more than allegiance to Notre Dame in common. Gerry admired Jim's courage. Jim enjoyed Gerry's spirit. They both relied on God. Gerry began calling him immediately after every Moeller game to report the score and recap the highlights. He visited him once a year. He told all of his friends about Jim and encouraged them to get to know him, too. Joe Paterno and Woody Hayes did.

"Jim's the most saintly man I've ever met in my life," Gerry said. "You know what he's told me? In all the years he's been afflicted, he never asked God why. That will humble you; that will make you become a better person. He's made me a better person."

Gerry's ability to relate to people, from janitors to bank presidents, is his greatest asset. He asks for help and everyone always says yes, because when they ask, Gerry never says no. There is always room for one more on his bus, in his locker room, or at his dinner table; always time to talk to one more person or to listen to what they have to say. He adopts people the way others adopt stray pets; he considers everyone his friend.

Bertie Whitney became his friend on a flight from Chicago to Cincinnati. Bertie was 88 years old at the time, a pensioner living in Maynard, Minnesota, on a monthly Social Security benefit of $273. Gerry was returning from a speech in Wisconsin, and Bertie was traveling to Kentucky to see his 90-year-old sister who was in poor health. Her son had sent him the plane ticket.

As Gerry would say, they just started shooting the breeze. For a man of 88, Bertie impressed Gerry as full of vitality. Despite living on such a meager fixed income, Bertie was a humble, pious, happy man. Bertie told Gerry he had been a school janitor before retirement; his son was now retirement age. Gerry listened to the old man talk about his life and thought to himself, "If God lets me live to be eighty-eight, I hope I'm as good a man as this man is." They talked and laughed all the way to Cincinnati.

"Hey, this has been a real pleasure," Gerry said to Bert. "Here's ten bucks so you can have a little spending money."

Bert was surprised and very appreciative.

"Here, give me the ten back," Gerry said. "Here's fifty."

Bert protested. "No, no, no. I can't."

"I made a lot of money today," Gerry said. "I wouldn't do this unless I wanted to. I want you to have a good time back there."

Bertie wrote Gerry a thank-you note. His neighbors wrote to Gerry, too, to tell him that Bert was one of the pillars of their community. Gerry answered Bert's note, and they began to correspond regularly. From time to time Gerry included another 10 or 20 dollars in his letters. "I'm getting more out of it than Bert is," he said.

This man who reaches out to people so eagerly is, at the same time, a demanding disciplinarian who rants at his players when they do not perform. He expects concentration and execution—

"Everybody's gotta do their job"—and screams loudly when either is missing. In his sharpest rebuke, though, he never utters a profanity or an insult. He forgives and forgets quickly, and looks for a reason to hug or joke with the player he has just chewed out. It is an effort for him to be so tough, but he knows that to ease up is to invite failure. The game must always be played on his terms.

When two prized underclassmen on the 1980 squad, halfbacks Hiawatha Francisco and Barry Larkin, were chosen to play for an all-star knothole baseball team in a tournament that could have extended into summer football practice, Gerry enforced a hard-nosed rule that required them to choose between the two sports.

"If the team a boy has played for all summer goes into tournaments," Gerry explained, "he can play until his team is eliminated. He's excused from football practice for that. But once his team is eliminated, he is not excused from even one day of football to play in any all-star games or for any all-star teams in tournaments. If a boy plays baseball for an all-star team after football starts, he can't play football at Moeller."

Gerry presented the choice to the mothers of both boys in successive phone calls one morning. He was at his persuasive best.

"Hello, Mrs. Francisco? Gerry Faust. Mrs. Francisco, I just want to explain our summer baseball rule to you so you can help Hiawatha decide whether he's going to play for that all-star team or play football at Moeller this year." He described the rule very quickly and added: "Mrs. Francisco, the schools with great programs have this rule. The mediocre teams don't have rules like that, and that's why they're mediocre. It's Hiawatha's choice, but I want to tell you the truth. His future is in football, not baseball. I know he thinks he's a great baseball player, but I've seen him, and he's not a baseball player. Now, Barry Larkin's future probably is in baseball, but Hiawatha is going to be a football player. Thanks, Mrs. Francisco. Tell Hiawatha we expect him here every day starting Tuesday if he's going to play football for Moeller this year."

Barely catching his breath, Gerry dialed again.

"Hello, Mrs. Larkin? Gerry Faust." Again a quick explanation of the baseball rule. "We have to have rules, Mrs. Larkin. I can't make exceptions for a couple at the expense of the other ninety. Mike Cameron, our baseball coach, even agrees with the rule the way it is now. I'll be honest with you, Mrs. Larkin. I think Barry's future is in baseball. But you're going to want Barry to go to college before he starts playing pro baseball, aren't you? They don't give many baseball scholarships; if Barry's going to get any help with his college expenses, it will probably be a football scholarship. His future's in baseball, but I don't see what difference a few more games at the end of summer will make. And it will be harder for him to get any aid in football if he doesn't play this year. But it's your choice."

Gerry challenges young people with hard decisions, teaching them to think and requiring them to be responsible for their actions. No one was spared these precious lessons, including a "special" young man he invited to serve as a student manager one season.

Doug was 19 and had a brother who was also a football manager for Gerry. Being a football manager was a prestigious assignment at Moeller; dozens of boys signed up for manager tryouts, and the best 16 were chosen to carry out the thankless dirty work associated with keeping the team running. Doug was honored when Gerry, on the day they met, asked him if he'd like to be a manager with his brother. Doug worked hard and had the time of his life. Everyone enjoyed seeing him enjoy himself so. Once, though, when Doug started slacking off a little, Gerry decided it was Doug's turn to learn one of life's hard lessons.

Doug had been excitedly telling a couple of coaches about a dance he was planning to attend the coming weekend. He marched up to Gerry with a glint in his eye and a smile on his face and reminded Gerry it was payday. His salary for keeping the weight room clean was $5 a week.

"I can't pay you anything this week," Gerry barked. "You didn't earn it."

Doug recoiled. "What do you mean?"

"You didn't do your job, Doug. You didn't clean the weight room."

"Yes I did—"

"No, Doug. The weight room isn't clean. There are weights lying all around. And you haven't swept the floor. You haven't been working around here at all lately, Doug. You're not doing your job. I asked you to help Mr. Becker, and you didn't do that either. I can't pay you when you don't do your job."

Doug was on the verge of a torrent of tears. His face cracked a little more as he absorbed each verbal blow.

"Mr. Faust," he stammered. "Can I say something?"

"Yes, Doug. Go ahead."

"Mr. Faust, I did help Mr. Becker when you told me to. Ask him. And I did clean the weight room. I'll clean it again if you want me to. I promise I'll do a good job from now on."

Doug was sniffling as he finished. Gerry reached into his pocket and pulled out a wrinkled five-dollar bill.

"All right, Doug. But remember—you have to do your job just like everybody else."

Doug was still quaking as he walked away. Gerry had been hard on him; he had almost gone too far. He made his point, to be sure, then compassion took over.

"Doug," he called out. "What's this I hear about you going to a dance this weekend? If you're going out on a date, you're going to need more than five dollars. Here's another five dollars for helping Mr. Becker."

Being a Moeller football player required considerable sacrifice. Dating was out of the question for most players until after the season; from August through November there was barely enough time to practice, sleep, attend class, and study. With various off-season training programs, football was a year-round proposition. The hardest time of year, without question, was summer practice, when the boys would arrive at 8 in the morning and stay until 6 in the evening, practicing twice a day in the scorching heat. High school players in Ohio were permitted to participate in three preseason scrimmages, but Gerry managed to schedule more than three by splitting his varsity into two squads.

Even Moeller's second team provided worthy competition, as a letter from Don Ross, the athletic director at Springboro High, located near Dayton, indicated:

I wanted to thank you for agreeing to scrimmage our kids. The scrimmage—even though it was against your second- and third-liners—did much to advance our football program. As a former head football coach, I was impressed with your team's decorum, techniques, and abilities. They are well-coached, well-disciplined, and, probably most importantly, sportsman-like. As you saw, a good portion of our community turned out for the scrimmage, mainly to see the Moeller legend. That turnout included people who have never been to a regular season game in our fifteen-year football history. The game itself gave our kids insight into what makes a winner: clean play, attention to detail, and innovative offense and defense. Best wishes for another state championship.

The drive to win another state championship was the undercurrent in every season after Moeller's first state title in 1975. Less than two weeks before the first game of 1980, however, a pair of newspaper headlines painted a new backdrop for what proved to be Gerry's last season at Moeller. The bold, black harbingers read:

Devine Announces He'll Retire After '80 Season
Faust Leaves Door Open On Notre Dame Candidacy

THE END OF AN ERA

GAME ONE: MOELLER vs. CENTERVILLE

August 29, 1980

Preseason practice ended on a successful note. A high society dinner-dance for the benefit of Moeller High School, specifically to help pay for the new athletic facility behind the school, cleared $170,000—possibly a record in the Cincinnati fund-raising league. More than 800 people paid $250 per person to honor Henry Gallenstein, a benefactor of youth for whom the new building expediently was named and who, on the Friday night following his fete, attended the first Moeller game of his life.

CBS was on hand as Moeller's student body reported for the first day of classes. The network crew stayed a week, shooting 13,000 feet of film for a Saturday afternoon documentary that was held until the last week of the season. Producer Cathy Olian, hardly a football expert herself, had read about Moeller in *Time* the preceding fall, just after the heralded Catholic school had won its fourth Ohio state championship in the previous five years. "They made Moeller sound great, but I wasn't sure. Everyone has a tendency to make their subjects sound better than they are, just to make the story better." She assembled a story proposal and asked her secretary to type it up, still wondering. "Some guy from accounting walked by, saw the name of the school in my proposal and said, 'Moeller High! Wow! They're the greatest high school football team ever!'" That convinced Cathy Olian.

The approaching season opener was forgotten, for a day, when Gerry confirmed the ominous implications of a quietly passed state athletic association rule change prohibiting a school from dressing more than 60 players for any state playoff game. For defending champion Moeller, it would mean 16 players who dressed all season would be stripped of their colors in the games they worked so hard to reach. Gerry immediately called Columbus, as he did whenever he and the Ohio High School Athletic Association (OHSAA) disagreed.

"I can't understand these people," he grumbled to his staff. "And they say they're for kids. We'll have sixteen guys who will have helped this team all season, who will have worked as hard as all the other guys—and I'm supposed to tell them they can't dress for the playoffs! The OHSAA can tell those kids; I sure won't!" Asked about the Centerville game, less than 48 hours away, Gerry shrugged. "I'm more concerned with this right now." Frowning, he burst forth with spiteful strategy. "I know what I'll do! I'll dress the other sixteen and buy them seats in the stands. And, during the game, we'll send kids from the field to the stands and from the stands to the field—all in uniform. That'll make our point!" His assistants brought Gerry back to the moment at hand: "Uh, Gerry," they reminded, "we have to *make it* to the playoffs, first."

Centerville was to prove a formidable opening opponent. While Moeller was winning 57 games and losing only one during the previous five seasons, Centerville, a coeducational public school of 3,000 students located near Dayton, Ohio, was winning 47 and losing three—missing the state playoffs three times as runner-up to Moeller in the region's computer ratings. The two varsities had never met, but two years earlier Centerville's sophomores had defeated the Moeller sophomores; 21–14. Those players were the seniors in this game, and, in the Moeller locker room, that sophomore score was printed on many signs and imprinted on many minds.

"Men," intoned assistant coach Paul Smith, just before the players boarded the bus for the ride to the stadium: "I never told anyone this before . . . but I overheard one of Centerville's best players talking to his dad as he walked off the field after that game two years ago. His dad said, 'See, Son, Moeller isn't so tough after all; are they!' And the boy said, 'No, Dad, Moeller's not so tough.' Men, here's your chance to show them how tough you are."

Even in the sport and the spirit of The Gipper, it was too good to be true. But later, Smitty affirmed that the conversation between father and son really did take place. And, it was Centerville's star, Gary Alders, maybe the best quarterback in the state, doing the talking.

From the time they gathered, three hours before game time, to the time they went their separate ways, about two hours after the game, Gerry and his team prayed together, aloud, on 14 occasions. It was that way every game. But, if religion mixed with football at Moeller, so, too, did football mix with religion. It was during the team chapel service that senior Ron Lindhorst spoke to his teammates about the season at hand:

"This is the first game of the thirteen-week season," he began. (It is 13 weeks *only* if a team advances to the state finals.) "We have been taught everything that could be taught; now, it is our turn. Remember every time you ran around that track; it formed you more and more. All of that goes into being a state champ. Summer practice was tough, but we made it. We are the Men of Moeller! We are the Moeller Family. There is nothing like that family in the country; everyone is for everyone, and that's what will make us a state champ. . . .

"Seniors: we have been through a lot, a loss to LaSalle and Centerville. That has to be the worst feeling, knowing you yourself let down and the whole team suffered. Everyone went home and looked in the mirror and wondered: Did they play their hardest? Centerville has wanted us since they beat us. During that game, I stood on the sideline wondering why I wasn't playing, but it was my own fault. I felt more hurt than anyone out there, because I couldn't do anything. So, this is my game and my season, because I am a senior. And, I want to become a champ. Good luck, Moeller! Beat Centerville!"

Ron Lindhorst had gone into summer practice as the starting quarterback, but came out a tight end. He was a good athlete who performed better, in the opinion of the coaching staff, when he was not facing the constant pressure of taking every snap. In a few hours he would star at his new position, in the too-good-to-be-true tradition of the famed Frank Merriwell or Chip Hilton.

On the 50-yard line, moments before the opening kickoff, Barry Sollenberger of the National Sports News Service, headquartered in Phoenix, Arizona, presented Moeller its 1979 national championship trophy. As Sollenberger admitted, there is more logic than science to his selection of a national high school champion.

"It's impossible to know who the best high school team in the nation really is, because you don't play each other on the field. They don't even know who the best college team is, for the same reason. But, I'll tell you this; the best high school football states are California, Ohio, Texas, Illinois, and Pennsylvania. And no other school has dominated any of those states the way Moeller has dominated Ohio football the last five years. It's the consistency that makes Moeller the best."

The trophy presentation was to have been the highlight of Moeller's first pep rally of the season, but alas, when the moment arrived, Sollenberger had not. Unaccustomed to seeing his promotions fail, a distraught Gerry Faust began his pep talk with an embarrassed apology. "We have this man come all the way from Phoenix, Arizona, to present the trophy at this pep rally . . . and then we forget to pick him up and bring him to the school! We, as coaches, failed you."

A football coach of 10 years, Cliff Martin, accompanied Sollenberger on his visit. Martin eagerly but stoically surveyed the Moeller machine and was surprised. "I expected to see eighty of the finest high school specimens in Ohio. But these are just like all other high school kids. There are skinny kids, fat kids, and some real studs. This team doesn't have a special bunch of athletes; they win with fantastic organization and coaching. These are college coaches, and this is a college program."

The game itself, as one of Moeller's 24 team doctors mused during the tense fourth quarter, was a "great game, an interesting game—something you don't see on this sideline that often." Centerville scored first, and Gary Alders was outstanding until he went out near halftime with a knee injury that, sadly, interrupted his senior season for several weeks. Ron Lindhorst caught two touchdown passes at his new position, and Moeller won, 20–14. The game was in doubt until the final minute. Fans stormed the field at the end, and it was some time before Gerry and his team could form a huddle, once again to pray. Elbowing his way through the crowd, Gary Alders approached.

"Great game, coach," he said bravely. "Take it all the way, you guys! Win state again!" Given a wrenching hug by Gerry, the boy left in tears.

"Our Lady of Victory," Gerry called out from the center of the huddle.

"Pray for us," answered the football team.

2

Growing Up to Be a Coach

In the coaching profession, Fuzzy Faust was something of a legend himself. He built a powerhouse at Dayton Chaminade High School that endured for most of three decades. Starting in an era when the head coach was the only coach, Fuzzy won roughly three fourths of the 200 or so games he coached. Gerry advanced from student manager to starting quarterback for the Chaminade team—with no special favors and few compliments from his dad.

Theirs was a good Catholic family. Fuzzy's wife stayed home, because she felt she should be there whenever her children needed her. They would come in, and, first thing, call, "Mother." And she would always answer, "I'm here." She was a slight woman, soft-spoken and slow to anger, but no pushover; she was the perfect complement to her husband. He was a good man, honest and hard-working and a fine example for their children; but he was strict and stern, the disciplinarian of the household. He held an engineering degree and worked part-time as a draftsman. His full-time occupation was teacher and coach.

Fuzzy and Alma Faust had three children. Their youngest boy was a natural athlete; football, baseball, golf, tennis—you name it. Even fishing and distance running; he was good at everything. He became a dentist. Their only daughter was a beautiful girl with blond hair. She was studious and a willing participant in school activities; even with her many interests, she still was a straight-A student. She became an interior designer, married a thoracic surgeon, and lives in Dayton in a veritable mansion, with swimming pool and tennis court. The oldest child, another boy, did not possess either his brother's prowess or his sister's diligence. Rheumatic fever at age five left him with a peculiar gait, almost a shuffle, and in grade school he had to put a rock in his left hand during calisthenics just so he could remember left from right. He was full of mischief, an irrepressible lad who confounded his industrious sister with his ability to prepare for tests in a few hours when it would take her a whole night. He became a football player, thanks largely to unwavering determination, and then a coach—eventually Notre Dame's coach.

The Fausts and their three children, Gerry, Marilee, and Freddie, lived modestly in a neighborhood known as Riverdale on the north side of Dayton, Ohio. Mrs. Faust hunted bargains, mended clothes, and made ends meet. She kept a spotless house, and there was a lot of love within. It was a close family.

When Christmas came, Mr. Faust would sell Christmas trees to pay for the presents. Young Gerry was in the fifth grade, and Marilee in the fourth, when dad asked for the first time if they would like to help. So, every day after school, Gerry and his little sister sold trees at the gas station across the street from their home. Gerry proved to be quite a salesman; in his first year, he moved 50 trees and cleared $150. The next year, the Fausts went into the Christmas tree business on their own, and bought their first television set with the profits. They defrosted the trees in their basement, to Mrs. Faust's chagrin, and worked around the clock. Even seven-year-old Freddie got to help.

Riverdale was a tough neighborhood; and fearless, adventurous young Gerry was ever ready to test it—even as a second grader against bullies from the third and fourth grades. He fought them for awhile but was outnumbered, so he ran. He tripped over a picket fence and one of the spikes went through his leg; the bullies went the other way. It was two blocks to home, and when Gerry arrived he went straight upstairs to his room.

"Mom, I can't walk."

"Gerry! What happened?"

Good ole Doc Duchak looked at the wound a short time later. "We can give you gas and you're going to be sick for a day or so," he said, "or we can do it without gas, which will hurt a lot more."

"Do it without gas," Gerry said. "I don't want to be sick." In the firm but tender grip of his father, seven-year-old Gerry gritted his teeth and took 11 stitches. He never forgot the four bullies, or the security he felt looking into his father's eyes. By the time he was in the eighth grade, he had licked each of the four in a fight—one on one, fair and square.

Gerry broke his share of the neighbors' windows, as boys sometimes do. And, he was not above grabbing onto the bumper of a passing car in winter and enjoying a brief tow through the snow, his clodhoppers serving as skis. Old Mrs. Kappeler, who lived across the street, was sure "that boy" was going to wind up in state prison.

Piano lessons lasted one visit; playing the piano was chicken. He chafed at the thought of dancing lessons, too; all that bow and dip stuff was for girls. But he had no choice; his mother walked him to class each week and turned him over to the teacher so he could not sneak off to a movie. His mother felt compelled to check with the nuns at school on a regular basis, too, just to be sure he was behaving himself.

Sister William Marie had her hands full with the fifth grade class. Besides Gerry Faust, she had to contend with Judy Hines, a devilish little tomboy who tried to match him prank for prank. One day, Judy had placed a tack on the seat in front of her. Gerry clomped in and plopped down. Then jumped up. Then turned around. Then retaliated. Sister William Marie came running and hit him with her ruler. She broke it and yelled, "You made me commit a mortal sin of anger!"

Sister Dismas, the principal, got her turn in the eighth grade. As principal, Sister Dismas had other responsibilities. She would be called out of class occasionally to meet a book salesman or to accept delivery of pencils, paper, and chalk. It was her duty, also, to dismiss the school at recess, lunchtime, and the end of the day. She did so by ringing a cowbell, then dispatching a student to ring it throughout the building. When Sister was called out of her room one afternoon, playful Gerry and an equally devious chum, who grew up to be a surgeon, looked out the window, admired the day, and decided it would be nice if they could leave a little early. One held the chair while the other advanced the clock's minute hand. Unsuspecting Sister Dismas returned, grabbed the cowbell, and dismissed the whole school 30 minutes early. The boys laughed all the way home, but the girls in the class squealed, and the perpetrators washed windows for a week.

Growing up in a Catholic school, and being the rambunctious sort, Gerry spent a considerable amount of time in the confessional.

Father Steincamp, in fact, got so he could tell when Gerry was coming. Commotion replaced silence in the church. One Holy Week, for example, the church was being repainted and the confessionals had been replaced temporarily with curtains hung in the aisle. Ten or twelve sinners waited in line. It was Gerry's turn. He stepped forward and jerked the curtain aside to enter the makeshift confessional. There was noise, a roar, as curtains and pipes collapsed. Gerry was buried under a pile of draperies. There was laughter in the church, and then a voice was heard.

"That could be only one kid," Father Steincamp bellowed. "Gerry Faust."

Gerry remembers his childhood whenever his own sons exasperate their mother, their teachers, or the neighbors, and he tempers his discipline with a chuckle kept to himself: "There I was, years ago." And when his wife, embarrassed over a binge of doorbell-ringing, says, "*You* wouldn't have done that when you were their age," he simply doesn't bother to answer.

Just down the street from the Fausts' home in Dayton was an orphanage, Shawn Acres. Gerry was best friends with Moses and Mouse and a lot of great guys who lived at Shawn Acres. They played football and baseball together and went swimming and to the movies. Shawn Acres had the only swimming pool in the neighborhood, and the orphans were treated to a movie at the Dale every Saturday. Gerry repaid the guys at Shawn Acres with special treatment when he got a job as a soda jerk at Meyers' Drug Store. No free drinks, just extra-thick shakes for the boys from the orphanage. Old Doc Meyers would look over his glasses every time he heard that machine mixing another shake. His patience ran out as summer ended.

"I think it would be in my best interest if you didn't come back next year," Gerry was told.

Gerry the organizer and Gerry the promoter flourished in the fourth grade. Cut from a knothole baseball team, he showed his hustle by forming a team of his own, the Riverdale Rats. He put the pinch on local merchants, then shopped the nearest sporting goods store for green and white shirts (the colors of his dad's Chaminade teams). He would walk into a store, dicker for the lowest price because he had only so much money, and come away with everything he needed. The Rats played the Siebenthaler Saints, the Hillcrest Hellions, and other collections of knothole rejects.

Gerry's baseball career, inauspicious as it was, ended in grade school. He made only one hit in two years. It came against Tom Travis, a boy who was so big he was not allowed to play grade school football. Tom Travis threw hard. Gerry just closed his eyes, swung, and got a single. He could not believe it. The next time up to bat, a pitch from Travis hit him in the head and knocked him out.

Convinced that his future was not in baseball, Gerry and his dad were faced with a major decision when Gerry started high school: What position would he try to play on Fuzzy's formidable football team?

Gerry weighed only 98 pounds, and he had no natural athletic ability. "He doesn't have enough speed to be a running back," his father thought. "He isn't big enough to be a lineman, and he isn't shifty enough to be an offensive end. There's only one place left for him to go. He's good with his hands and he has brains. I'll try him at quarterback."

Gerry and Freddie hung a tire on a rope, and Gerry threw passes for hours at a time. He worked all summer. Nevertheless, Fuzzy cut him the first day! Gerry did not speak to his father for several days, then decided to show his dad he could make himself a football player. He became a student manager and learned to appreciate those indispensable helpers. He watched every move the varsity quarterbacks made, too, and eventually became the best play-calling and ball-handling quarterback Fuzzy Faust ever coached. He made the team as a sophomore, fourth-string quarterback. That summer he worked at a soft drink plant, lifting cases onto delivery trucks. At night he ran a mile up and down hills. He grew five inches and gained almost 40 pounds. He came back to Chaminade for his junior year standing five feet eleven and weighing 162 pounds. He was third-string starting out.

Playing for his father was never easy. Fuzzy Faust was more demanding of his son than any other player. Gerry had to be twice as good, and even then he should not expect compliments. Fuzzy knew his boy had limited ability; he did not want anyone hurting his feelings by suggesting he was getting special favors.

"Remember," he told Gerry more than once, "you're the coach's son, and everybody's going to say you're playing because you're the coach's son. It's not going to work out that way."

This attitude worried Gerry's mother. "You're going to break his spirit," Alma Faust said many times to her husband. "He won't like you. You'll get him so that he'll hate you."

But Fuzzy would not let up. Just before the season opener in

Gerry's junior year, he met with his assistant coach, John Spezzaferro, to discuss the starting lineup. Spez wanted to start the coach's son at quarterback.

"I'll go along with you on every position, John, except Gerry at quarterback," Fuzzy said.

"Gerry's a better quarterback than the other two fellows," Spez argued.

"There's no way I'm starting that kid—that's my son, and if I start that kid and things go wrong, they're all going to say he's in there because he's my son."

"You're making a big mistake," Spez retorted.

"That's the way it's going to be."

Gerry fidgeted on the sidelines through three quarters of the game. The Chaminade offense was not moving the ball. When he finally entered the game, Chaminade was losing 7–0. He quarterbacked a touchdown, but his team still lost 7–6.

The next week Spezzaferro again wanted to start Gerry at quarterback; again Fuzzy Faust said no. And, again Chaminade fell behind 7–0. Gerry entered the game in the second quarter, and Chaminade came to life behind him. Still, his stubborn father refused to stick with him when the second half started. The crowd began to boo the coach. Some people shouted, "Put Gerry in. Let him play." Those were the words Fuzzy Faust was waiting to hear. Gerry played the rest of the game and the rest of the season. Chaminade scored four touchdowns in the second half and won 32–7. The opening game was the team's only loss all year.

Starting at quarterback was no longer an issue when Gerry returned for his senior year, but father coaching son remained a challenge to their relationship, at least as outsiders saw it. There were times when Gerry would not speak to his father for days. Only once did he complain, though.

"Do you have to be so tough on me?" he asked one night as they rode home together.

"Didn't I tell you when you came out that that's the way it was going to be if you played for me?" his father snapped.

Gerry's teammates actually grew closer to him for it. They thought nothing of confiding in him, telling secrets they would not tell most coach's sons, and inviting him to parties and places where a coach's son might not have been welcome. They nominated him to be their captain in one memorable locker room meeting.

Gerry at age 5 in 1940. The C on his sweater stands for Chaminade, the team coached by his father. *Faust family album.*

Gerry plays center with younger brother Fred as the halfback in 1947. Their sister, Marilee, holds the family dog, Bingo. *Faust family album.*

Although he weighed only 155 pounds, Gerry was an all-state quarterback during his senior year in high school. *Faust family album.*

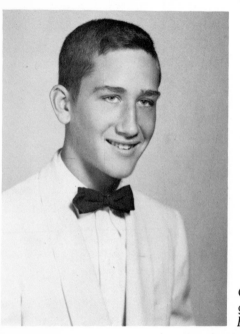

Gerry's high school graduation picture in 1953. *Faust family album.*

Gerry as a senior at the University of Dayton in 1958. *Faust family album.*

Gerry with his parents, Fuzzy and Alma Faust, on New Year's Day 1981.
Faust family album.

Family portrait. Gerry with wife Marlene and their three children: Gerry, at
left; Julie, at right, and Steve, at rear. *Faust family album.*

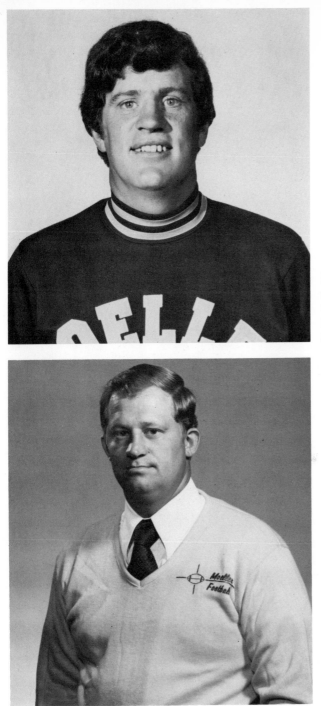

Mike Cameron, new Moeller athletic director, worked with Gerry as the defensive backfield coach. *Moeller High School photo*.

Ted Bacigalupo succeeded Gerry as Moeller's head football coach. *Moeller High School photo*.

Meetings of the Moeller football staff were crowded affairs. This discussion involves 14 of Gerry's 17 assistant coaches. *Photo by Michael E. Keating*.

Jeff Leibert, head freshman coach at the height of the Faust era, was promoted to assistant athletic director. *Moeller High School photo.*

Line coach Jim Higgins prepared players with sideline chalk talks throughout every Moeller game. Higgins went to Notre Dame with Faust. *Moeller High School photo.*

Whenever Fuzzy Faust attended a Moeller game, Gerry insisted he spend a few moments on the field. Head basketball coach Dave Hammer, also a football assistant, is behind Fuzzy. *Photo by Ed Reinke.*

Moeller High would sell 10,000 football tickets before the first day of school.
Photo by Michael E. Keating.

"We've got to name a captain for today," Fuzzy Faust announced to his team.

Bob Staley got up. "We'd like to have Gerry as captain." Gerry perked up. He was honored. He wanted to be their captain.

"No. Gerry wouldn't like it, and I wouldn't like it," Fuzzy said. "It's not the right thing to do. We'll name someone else captain."

After eight successive victories, Chaminade was scheduled to end the season with games against heralded Chicago Mount Carmel and the best team in Cincinnati, Purcell. Mount Carmel was coached by Terry Brennan, who two years later became the youngest head coach Notre Dame has ever had. Chaminade lost, 28–21, in one of the greatest high school football games ever played in Dayton. The next week's game was even better. It was the end of Faust & Faust, and what an end it was. Purcell was leading, 21–7 at the half, when Fuzzy dropped his bombshell. He was retiring after this game. Not even his son knew it was coming. The kids started to cry, Gerry included. It was time to return to the field. Sixteen thousand fans had jammed Xavier University's stadium expecting one of Cincinnati's best high school football games ever. They were not cheated. Chaminade stormed ahead with three touchdowns. Purcell scored late, and Gerry's last high school game ended in a 27–27 tie. As they left the field, Fuzzy hugged Gerry and said, simply: "Thanks."

A couple of weeks later Fuzzy was interviewed by Dayton *Daily News* sports editor Si Burick. Gerry had been named all-city quarterback by both Dayton newspapers and was recognized as a third-team all-stater.

"It's been tough over the last two years," Fuzzy was quoted, "because I've never said anything to him. But I'd have to rank him up there as one of the best quarterbacks I've ever had."

Gerry had to read the sports page to learn of such praise, but he looks back on the whole experience and says, "I wouldn't trade it for anything. I got to play for the greatest high school football coach who ever lived."

Gerry was recruited by Xavier, Ohio University, Dayton, Indiana, Harvard, and Notre Dame. He really wanted Notre Dame; he had dreamed of playing for the Fighting Irish since grade school. He was invited to South Bend for a workout back when on-campus tryouts were still permitted. He still remembers the experience.

Gerry walked into the fieldhouse, and a man shouted, "Quarterbacks over here." There were 19 studs in line to take a turn throwing the ball. Len Dawson and Paul Hornung, he was told, were among them. Awed by what he was seeing, Gerry thought, "Holy mackerel! What am I doing here?" When his turn came, he said to the coach running the tryout, "Sir, you don't really want to see me throw."

Notre Dame offered a partial scholarship, though Gerry was sure it was only because he was Fuzzy Faust's son. A partial was not enough; Gerry's family could not make up the difference. When the Notre Dame recruiter called back, Gerry had to turn him down.

"I can't play up there," he said. "I don't have the ability to play in that league. It's a great school, a great university, and I really appreciate the honor of being offered a partial. I think it's an honor just to even take a visit up there. Thanks a million."

Gerry signed with Ohio University (not to be confused with Ohio *State* University). He had an offer from the University of Dayton, but his dad did not like the coaching staff. Gerry lasted one semester at Ohio U. He was homesick and transferred to his hometown school. By then, Hugh DeVore, later to coach Notre Dame and the Philadelphia Eagles, had become the University of Dayton's coach. As a transfer, Gerry was ineligible to play for one year. He served as a member of the rat squad—the punching bags for the guys who play. Eight days into his first summer practice—stuck at defensive end—Gerry was ready to quit. He called home and told his dad he'd had enough. He was getting killed at defenisve end; he was not a defensive player.

"You do what you want to do," his dad said. "I don't want to stand in your way. But, when you come home, you've got to pay your own way to school, and don't you ever ask me for anything out of the ordinary, because I don't like quitters."

Gerry went to an assistant coach, Stan Zadel, who convinced him to at least finish summer practice. Only seven more days. Gerry agreed. Three days later a quarterback was injured, and Gerry moved over to the offense. He is eternally grateful to Stan Zadel.

It was at Dayton that Gerry met Jim Katcavage, who later played defensive end on some of the New York Giants' greatest teams. Theirs was a rugged friendship. Though he was best at fakes, handoffs, and short passes, Gerry had to run the option play, too, at Dayton. Every time around the end, Kat was waiting. Every time, a punishing hit. Every time, Gerry would bounce up, smiling. Gerry respected Kat for his greatness; Kat respected Gerry for his determination. But once, when Kat went too far, in Gerry's opinion, his Riverdale childhood told him not to let the defensive end get away with it. Five plays later, Gerry decked him—a perfectly legal forearm.

"That will be the last time you take a cheap shot at me," he said with bravado. Kat didn't say a word. "Boy, I called his bluff," Gerry thought.

A little later, standing near a pileup *after* the whistle, Gerry's lights went out. Hit from behind, he was carried off the field with torn cartilage in one knee. He thought, "If I ever get that Kat, I'll kill him!" Gerry was through for the rest of the spring practice.

Katcavage was the first player to visit him. While Gerry limped around on crutches, the big guy carried his books. He took good care of Gerry.

"Kat," Gerry asked, "why did you do that to me?"

Katcavage said, "I don't take anything from anybody on the field."

"Okay," Gerry said. Just the kind of guy you want on your side.

It was not all work and no play in college. The fun-loving side of Gerry actually added a new dimension—dating. It was an up-coming college dance that inspired Gerry to attempt one of his most outlandish stunts. Eight guys shared a house during his days at Dayton. They were sitting around, talking about the approaching dance and discussing dates.

"You know," said Gerry, "you could really take two dates to the dance and get by with it."

"No, you can't."

"You wanna bet?"

If anyone could pull it off, it was Gerry. He had a reputation for bringing a date to a party, sitting her down with friends, and going around talking with everyone there. He danced with his girl and treated her right, whoever she was that night, but she knew going in that she was going to sit for a time while Gerry said hello to everybody. For this caper, Gerry lined up a nurse, because nurses had a 1 o'clock curfew, and a coed who lived at home in Dayton; she had no curfew. Lakeside Ballroom was a big place, seating perhaps 3,000 people. Half of Gerry's buddies agreed to sit at one end of the place, the rest at the opposite end. About twenty bucks rode on the outcome.

Gerry arrived with the nurse, quickly sat her down with the

guys at the far end, and said, "Well, I'm going to say hello to everybody." He was back in his car in a flash and drove to the other girl's home. He had chosen her because she lived near the ballroom. When they arrived at the dance, Gerry's friends were saving him seats right in front. How nice of them. There were 700½ couples at the dance. Gerry and his two dates had a lovely time. Things were going great, but word got out. As Gerry crossed the dance floor again and again, the guys started cheering. He was going to pull it off. His buddies, though, decided to have some fun of their own. "Don't go home when Gerry asks you to," they told the girls. "He wants to go out with some guys, and he's going to tell you he doesn't feel well. Make him stay with you."

Sure enough. "Hey, I don't feel very well," Gerry said to the nurse. "It's time to go home."

"I'm staying," she said. She had gotten her curfew waived for the night.

"Okay, we'll stay." He could always take the other girl home first, he thought. But she said the same thing.

The night ended with a friend and his date driving Gerry's car. In the back seat sat Gerry huddled between two angry young ladies giving him the cold shoulder. He sent them both flowers and sent the bill to his buddies who had sabotaged an otherwise perfect prank.

The Canadian Football League called when Gerry graduated. He was offered $3,200 as a rookie. He also had a partnership in an insurance agency right in Dayton, if he wanted it. That offered big money to start, maybe $7,000 a year. He turned down both jobs. He wanted to be a coach. The offer he was waiting for came quickly. Chaminade had an opening, and he jumped at it even though it was for considerably less money.

An old family friend, Brother Larry Eveslage, brought Gerry to Cincinnati two years later. Brother Eveslage had been athletic director at Chaminade during the 1930s. He worked with Fuzzy and watched Gerry grow up. His order, the Society of Mary, moved him around to Marianist schools in Cleveland and Cincinnati. But he always stayed in touch with the Fausts. When he visited them in spring 1960, he had been given a new assignment. A new school, Moeller High, would be opening in Cincinnati that fall, and he was going to be the principal. He needed a football coach.

"Do you think Gerry would be interested?" he asked Fuzzy.

There were more than 30 applicants for the job as Moeller's first football coach, but only one contender in the eyes of the first principal.

"I knew Gerry not only was raised on football," Brother Eveslage said years later, "but he also was a very intelligent fellow. I knew the Faust household; I knew he was a good Catholic kid. A football coach can have a tremendous influence on kids, and I wanted that to be a good Catholic influence."

THE END OF AN ERA

GAME TWO: MOELLER vs. CANTON McKINLEY

September 6, 1980

When the buses pulled up to the Pro Football Hall of Fame five hours before game time, three men were waiting. There was Sully Santucci, a kind old gentleman from Warren, Ohio, who once upon a time was as staunch a believer in northern Ohio football as you'll ever find, but was now "the president of the Moeller Fan Club in the North," Gerry proclaimed by way of introduction. And there was Lou Scott from Cleveland, a success in the Gerry Faust tradition, a businessman who started from scratch and built a hundred-million-dollar company in 15 years. And there was John Stoker, one of Gerry's first players and first converts to Catholicism; formerly a McKinley Boosters Club official, he served as Moeller's advance man for this trip. The Moeller entourage was always a large one, and, for each game, it included a few special guests. Santucci, Scott, and Stoker were to be a part of everything—the Hall of Fame visit, dinner, church services, pep talks, and the game itself, with guaranteed places in the locker room and along the sideline.

White-haired Sully Santucci abandoned his northern bias and became a Moeller believer about 1972, when he visited his daughter and grandchildren in Cincinnati. "I kept reading about this Moeller team that was supposed to be so great," he said. "I told my daughter I had to see for myself." Moeller and its opponent were unbeaten until the game Sully chose to see, and Moeller won by 40 points. Gerry welcomed him warmly, they became friends, and Sully went home convinced. "But all my friends laughed at me and said, 'Ah, what's this Moeller, Sully? They won't beat our northern teams.' But then Moeller started winning state championships. They don't laugh at me anymore. They call me 'Mr. Moeller.' And a lot of them have become Moeller fans, too." Sully regularly clipped area sports pages and sent the news of the north to Gerry.

Lou Scott met Gerry in Puerto Rico. It was March 1980, and Scott had hired him to speak at the annual convention of his company, Management Recruiters International. "He was our closing speaker, and he just laid them in the aisles. He got a ten-minute standing ovation. No one went out the side door—everyone went out the center aisle so they could shake hands with him." Friends in the business world had told Scott about the high school coach from Cincinnati who was fast becoming a popular business speaker, so he checked him out. "He was the first speaker I ever hired without hearing him first. IBM doesn't bring somebody back ten times unless he's good, and 3M doesn't bring people back unless they do a great job. Gerry Faust is probably one of the most sincere, caring, and loving human beings in the world today. That's what makes him such an effective speaker. What he says, he lives by." Lou Scott figures he has heard and hired the best, from Zig Ziegler down. "And I guarantee you," he said on the sideline in Fawcett Stadium, "Zig Ziegler wouldn't follow Gerry Faust on a program. He wouldn't do it."

John Stoker was a sophomore at Dayton Chaminade when Gerry began his coaching career there as an assistant. "He was always taking me to church," Stoker recalled, "always cornering me and trying to get me to convert. I wasn't Catholic. I went to Chaminade because most of my friends, who were Catholic, went there." In the years after Chaminade, Stoker married a Catholic girl and converted, moved to Canton, became a McKinley booster . . . and lost touch with Gerry Faust. They were reunited at the 1979 state championship game. "I was walking down the hallway to the Moeller locker room, and Gerry was being interviewed. He stopped the interview, pulled me alongside him, and introduced me to the press. He said, 'This is John Stoker. He used to play football for me.' It made me feel like a million dollars."

"When I came up to him," Stoker marveled, "you know the first thing he asked me? He wanted to know how my mother was! He hadn't seen my mother in twenty years, but he knew how close we were."

Moeller flew coaches to Canton twice to scout McKinley, and each time John Stoker chauffeured them. He sampled several eating establishments before recommending a cafeteria 10 minutes from the stadium, and he made the rounds of nearby churches to find one where Moeller could pray before the game. When Gerry made the last scouting trip, he checked out not only the McKinley football team but also Stoker's selections. The food was fine and the price was right, but the church was too far from the stadium.

John found another church. And, as a finishing touch, he greeted
Gerry at the Hall of Fame with a ready-made pre-game pep talk of
paragraphs clipped from the sports pages of the local paper.

Strolling through the Hall of Fame, the Moeller football team
was an impressive sight, more than 90 clean-cut young men all
saying, "Yes, sir," "No, sir," "Excuse me," "Please," and "Thank
you." All wore snappy two-button pullover Moeller sport shirts,
white with yellow breastplate and shoulders, trimmed with a "Moeller Blue" border around the sleeves and across the chest—as Gerry
would say, "first class." The stop at the Hall of Fame, of course, was
more than a mere diversion, more than a treat for the boys after a
long bus ride. There is something about watching Red Grange or
Gale Sayers run around and through bewildered tacklers, something about seeing those great Packer teams in action, or Joe
Namath and the Jets pulling that incredible upset, that gets a young
man ready to play the game himself. And it was no simple coincidence that the big TV in the lobby was blaring with live coverage of
Notre Dame's season opener, with a half dozen Moeller grads in
action for the Irish. It never hurts to remind high school football
players of their heritage before a particularly big game.

McKinley High School is located next door to the Hall of Fame,
and the football program's well-chosen motto is "Where Champions Are Made, *and* Success Is Tradition." McKinley's forerunner,
Canton High School, started playing football in 1894, and in 86
years and 762 games, the winning percentage of the "Red and
Black" is .710. There are two kinds of big games at Canton
McKinley—those involving Massillon, Canton's arch-rival for 84
years, and a few others against the rest of the world. There was no
mistaking that this one was about as big as a McKinley game can be
without involving the hated Massillon Tigers. McKinley's football
guide termed the game "the No. 1 attraction of the season." Early
in the week, McKinley coach Terry Forbes had closed practice and
declined to be interviewed. The McKinley Boosters staged their
annual spaghetti dinner, and for the first time in the history of
Fawcett Stadium, a McKinley game began with a fireworks display.
McKinley had lost to Moeller 14–2 in the 1977 state championship
game, and this was considered a rematch with honor at stake. The
crowd was 20,000, largest for any "non-Massillon" game in at least
eight years. It included a large group of Massillon fans who turned
out partly to root for McKinley's defeat and partly to check out

Moeller, a Massillon opponent in the 1981 regular season and possibly in the 1980 state playoffs. Massillon radio was even there for a pre-game interview with Coach Faust. "Do you recruit?" Gerry was asked point-blank. "We run the most honest program in the state," he answered calmly, but firmly.

Not all northern fans considered Gerry a suspicious success. Matthew Stephens of Dover stopped him outside the locker room just before the final fighting words were to be spoken and asked him to autograph two programs. "I saw him on TV once," he explained. "I liked the way he'd say something to the team, and then say a Hail Mary . . . say something to the team, and say another Hail Mary. That was nice—and I'm not even Catholic. Besides," the man added, "this might be a valuable autograph—he might be the next head coach at Notre Dame." Gerry obliged and thanked the man despite the timing, then entered the Moeller sanctuary and pulled out John Stoker's clippings.

> . . . many of the Moeller wins have come against teams, particularly in the early years, that are not the caliber of the McKinleys . . . The Cincinnati contingent will bus here today and return right after the game. Terry Forbes and Company would like very much to make it a long ride home for the Crusaders . . .

Lou Scott's eyes twinkled as Gerry switched to his own words.

"Men, it *was* a long ride up here. We came a long way to play a football game. It *can* be a *long* ride back, or it can be four-and-a-half hours of the joy and fun and satisfaction that come from winning! Mr. Sully Santucci can tell you: This isn't just McKinley versus Moeller; this is the north against the south! You're the best, and they're out to get you!"

The realistic McKinley fans at the spaghetti dinner conceded that Moeller was the favorite and surely would win. The hope, even among players' parents who worked the dinner, was that it would be close. But Moeller dominated the first quarter, and 16 minutes into the game held a 21–0 lead. McKinley played them even the rest of the way to lose, 34–14.

The long bus ride back to Cincinnati was a happy one, though interrupted less than halfway home. Gerry had forgotten to place the two telephone calls he makes after every game, and even though it was 1:30 in the morning, he had to find a phone. The bus driver exited the interstate at Mansfield. One call went to Jim Kennedy in Philadelphia; the other was to mom and dad in Dayton.

3

The Early Days of a Dynasty

The Greater Cincinnati League (GCL) celebrated its fiftieth anniversary in 1977, a union of Catholic boys high schools renowned for the excellence of its athletes and the ferocity of its interscholastic competition. "It is the best high school football league in the Midwest, and one of the best in the nation," recruiters from the Big Ten, Big Eight, and Atlantic Coast conferences routinely agree. Each year the best of these leagues battle major independents such as Penn State, Notre Dame, and the military academies for the GCL's best senior prospects. At least a dozen league players receive major college football scholarships each year; every major college conference in the nation has signed at least one GCL graduate; and the league averaged almost one pro player a year during the 1970s.

For the first 35 years of its existence, the GCL was a four-team league comprised of Elder, a school of 1,600 boys staffed by diocesan priests on the blue-collar west side; Roger Bacon, a Franciscan institution for 1,200 boys in the industrial central Millcreek Valley; Purcell, operated by the Marianists with a peak enrollment of 1,200 boys and located in a once-affluent neighborhood on the east side; and St. Xavier, a prep school run by the Jesuits for 1,200 college-bound students.

Through the years each school enjoyed its period of supremacy. Purcell's "Hackberry Street Assassins" dominated the 1940s and 1950s, though not without interruption. Roger Staubach graduated from Purcell in 1960, and Roger Bacon High, under Bron

Bacevich, the winningest high school football coach of all time (315 victories in 40 seasons) took over for most of the next decade.

For almost four decades the biggest high school event in Cincinnati was the annual GCL Doubleheader showcasing all four teams on a Sunday afternoon at Xavier University's stadium. But, as postwar babies began reaching high school age, and families began moving to the suburbs, more schools were needed. The Archdiocese of Cincinnati established LaSalle High School, to be staffed by the Christian Brothers in the northwest suburbs, and Moeller High School, the Marianists' second school, to the northeast. The league doubled in size by also adding a small coeducational school, McNicholas, located east of the city, and a Northern Kentucky boys' school, Newport Catholic.

LaSalle delayed starting football for a year, but Moeller, under the direction of Brother Eveslage, hired Gerry as its first football coach while the school was under construction. Football was important to Brother Eveslage, a large, athletic man who had taught at Purcell for 17 years.

"I was there during every glory year," he said. "I saw what football can mean to a school. A successful football team sets the tone for the whole year. If you win, you're great and everything in the school is great. If not, everything's different."

Gerry and Brother Eveslage discussed philosophy before Gerry accepted the job. "He wanted something the kids could rally around," Gerry recalls, "but he said it should never take charge of the school—above academics or discipline or moral training." Gerry's questions dealt with potential; he never mentioned salary. Was the district locked in, he wanted to know, or did it have room to grow? Would he be able to hire coaches? How many parishes were assigned to the school? What economic class would be going to the school? What part of town would it be drawing from?

"I had a philosophy," Gerry said 20 years later. "Middle-class kids. I thought you won with middle-class kids. I've changed that since I've been at Moeller. It's not the economic situation; it's the type of leadership at home. The Moeller district had the affluent middle class and the lower middle class—every economic class. And that's best. In a school that's structured in one economic class, the kid doesn't get a balanced education. Economic class is just as important as ethnic classes."

Moeller was blessed with good stock from the day its attendance boundaries were drawn by the archdiocese. "When Purcell was great," explained Brother Eveslage, "our best kids came from Norwood and Evanston. By the time the 1960s rolled around, Silverton, Rossmoyne, and Deer Park were being developed, and our best athletes were coming from there. Silverton, Rossmoyne, and Deer Park all became part of the new Moeller district." One of Roger Bacon's most productive territories was suburban Reading. That, too, became Moeller property, and 10 of Moeller's first 22 starters came from there—following a small rebellion. The parish of Sts. Peter and Paul in downtown Reading submitted a long petition to the archbishop asking that it remain a part of the Bacon district instead of being assigned to Moeller. "And they were only ten minutes away from the new school," Brother Eveslage noted with mirth. Twenty years later parents were moving across town to live in the Moeller district.

Gerry equipped the first Moeller team with hand-me-downs from a variety of sources. During summer practice that year, he helped the staffs of two Dayton public schools, Colonel White and Roosevelt, and they repaid the favor with some old football shoes. His alma mater, the University of Dayton, sold him old jerseys for two dollars apiece and gave him some old leather helmets and shoulder pads. He packed everything in a truck, and when he got to Reading, he got lost. He asked people how to get to Moeller High School, but they had never even heard of it. When Gerry arrived at Moeller, the old equipment smelled of mildew. "I was so excited," he says.

When he called the first Moeller team together for the first time, he used the positive approach. "You guys are lucky," he began. "We've got the best equipment for freshmen anywhere—college equipment!" At best, they had the best hand-me-downs. And, it was pretty obvious. For the first couple of years, the Blue and Gold of Moeller dressed in black jerseys and pants donated by the University of Cincinnati.

The team's first seven-man blocking sled was built by a carpenter and a plumber whose sons were trying out for the team. Both boys made it, of course. A two-man sled was bought for $225 and given to the school by the father of another player. Even the lockers were secondhand. St. Xavier was demolishing its downtown building after moving to a new suburban location. The lockers at the old school were going to be junked. Again, Moeller's young coach was excited. He borrowed another truck and drove downtown. For a day, the "Moeller Wrecking Crew" had a different meaning.

Moeller High had only two paid coaches at the start, Gerry and Bill Dailey, the first basketball coach. Dailey was Gerry's assistant, and Gerry was his. "Boy, did he get the short end of the deal," Gerry laughs. It was not long before Bill Clark and Carl Rahe showed up to help.

Bill Clark worked the cake mix line at Procter & Gamble for more than 20 years, making sure the chocolate or cherry or vanilla was added to the flour and eggs in just the right amounts. He played football for Wyoming High, a small suburban Cincinnati public school that during the 1950s and 1960s fashioned winning streaks of 43, 29, and 25 games. Bill's brother-in-law played on the first Moeller team, and Bill occasionally stopped by to watch practice. It reminded him of his own high school days, when the head coach was the only coach and an industrial arts teacher tried to help but knew nothing about football. Bill offered his services through a messenger.

"My brother-in-law asked if you need any help," defensive back Ed Baumann told Gerry one day. "He said he'd be glad to come over. He played some high school football and some college football, and he works the second shift at Procter & Gamble, so he can work his hours out so that he can be here in the afternoon."

Gerry said, "We'd be more than happy to have him," and Bill Clark joined the team in time for the first Moeller pep rally, an occasion he won't forget.

"Gerry led the Moeller cheer," Bill recalls, "and spelled it M-U-E-L-L-E-R."

For four years Bill Clark was Moeller's only offensive line coach, often coming to morning workouts during summer practice straight from an overtime shift. He turned over the basement of his home to the football team, too. "His greatest contribution to Moeller football was starting the weight program," Gerry says with reverence. It began innocently enough, about 15 or 20 kids, three times a week. Bill would be upstairs trying to sleep, listening to his weights clanging back and forth. It went on like that for more than 10 years. And, of course, it grew. By 1972, there were almost a hundred football players pumping iron in the Clarks' crowded basement, so Gerry and a bunch of his former players built a concrete block weight room near the practice field. Lettering over the door reads, "Bill Clark's Weight Room."

Brother Eveslage introduced Carl Rahe to Gerry, in a manner of speaking. "Carl, go around back and see what we've got out behind the school," he said. Carl, who had played football at Purcell when Brother Eveslage taught there, expected a hole in the ground for another building, or a piece of equipment or a statue of Mary. Instead, he saw Fuzzy Faust's kid drilling the first ragamuffin Moeller football team.

"I couldn't believe my eyes," Carl says. "He was a wild man."

Carl could have played college football, but his father urged him to learn a trade instead. So Carl became an auto mechanic and, inevitably, driver and keeper of the Moeller team bus; like everyone else, he found it impossible to say no to Gerry.

The first Moeller bus was a one-dollar bargain, purchased from a public school district that had given it up for dead. Carl made it run and kept it running for eight years. It was a big part of Moeller football's early history. When the fledgling Moeller Crusaders would return from a defeat, Gerry would tell Carl to drive straight up onto the practice field. Carl would aim the headlights across the field, and there, in the shadowy darkness, the determined neophytes would run laps and drill to correct the flaws that had just cost them a ball game. Gerry did not learn temperance for several years.

"Those kids had to be tough to go through what we put them through," he recalls with admiration. "I was unmerciful. I told them it wasn't because they lost, but because of the way they played. They accepted everything I did, and that laid the foundation of our tradition. I don't know how they did it."

The Moeller freshmen won four, lost four, and tied two in 1960. There were times when Gerry, expecting too much too quickly, talked of quitting. But he resisted the urge. As sophomores, the first Moeller graduating class lost just once, to the only varsity team they played, and won the GCL junior varsity championship. Moeller played its first varsity schedule in 1962, fielding a team made up solely of juniors and sophomores. The historic year was recorded for posterity by foresighted Brother Joseph Choquette, the athletic director.

Moeller lost its first varsity game, 16–6, to Hamilton Catholic. Brother Choquette declared it a moral victory in his notebook diary:

> The boys played a commendable game, naturally tense and shaky, but not scared. After kicking off and recovering a fumble, we passed on the first play. If completed, it was a sure T.D. However, we did score in the first series of downs. Missed E.P. In the second quarter an incompleted "flat pass" on the

seven-yard line killed our opportunity of sure victory. This was a good pass by Tom Kenny, but the receiver was too anxious. Everyone, including officials, commented on the fine play of our boys. Good, clean, hard football. We'll lose most of our games, but the boys will play good ball.

Brother Choquette ended his first entry with a prediction: "We'll be heard of. Wait till '63 and '64."

Moeller's first varsity victory came two weeks later, a 40–8 rout of nearby Deer Park High. "Boys are proving themselves to be a mature team," wrote Brother Choquette. "Coaching has much to do with it!" The next week Moeller played Elder, ranked third in the state, and lost 8–0. "What a beautiful game played by a freshman (Jim Davis), sophomores, and juniors," Brother Choquette noted in his journal. "Our boys are maturing unbelievably early!" Gerry, too, was encouraged by the performance. It was "the best game a Moeller team ever played," he announced on the team bus. "We're going to sing all the way home."

The young coach was taught an unforgettable lesson when Moeller ventured across the Ohio River to play Holmes High of Covington, Kentucky, the following weekend. The Bulldogs were coached by a gruff, paunchy curmudgeon respectfully and descriptively known as Bulldog Ellis.

Moeller had a great passing quarterback, Tom Kenny, and Holmes ran the ball all the time. But throughout the first half, Kenny was throwing terribly. Gerry could not understand it, and his quarterback could not explain it.

"Start throwing the ball! What's the matter with you!" Gerry screamed.

"Coach, I can't seem to grip the ball," the bewildered young athlete answered.

"Don't give me those excuses! Next time throw the ball!"

Holmes pulled ahead by two touchdowns. Gerry continued to yell at Kenny, who was not improving. At halftime, Gerry checked the game balls. Eight pounds of pressure in a 13-pound ball! Throwing a fully inflated football in the second half, Kenny passed for three touchdowns. But Moeller lost, 25–24.

The ninth game of the first varsity season was a 36–8 loss to Purcell. "A very tense game," recorded Brother Choquette:

The Purcell coach deliberately tried to run the score up! No success! More power to the coaches and team. With little more than thirty seconds left in the game and Purcell with the ball on our twenty-five, he called time for each play to get another T.D. We stopped them and took over with four or five seconds left. We'll remember this for '63.

A 44–20 victory over LaSalle completed the 1962 season with a record of four victories and six defeats. "A very successful first season—any way one looks at it!!" concluded Brother Choquette. "We'll go a long way next year."

Moeller's first senior team defeated three of the GCL's four established members and lost only once in 10 games, to powerful Roger Bacon. "I handled that game all wrong," Gerry tells everyone to this day. "I wanted to beat Bacon so bad, and I thought the way to do it was to get our kids really psyched up. We spent the whole week firing them up, and by game time they were so tight they couldn't move. They were shaking. I lost that game myself." The final score was 32–6. "I learned a valuable lesson from that game. You have to be very careful how you prepare a team. You can get kids *too* high."

Gerry believes Moeller was the better team that year, and a comparison of scores supports his contention. Roger Bacon defeated Purcell by only 6–0, while Moeller, as Brother Choquette had warned after the 1962 game, crushed Purcell. The final score was 54–0, "the worst defeat in Purcell's history," Brother Choquette noted. "We simply ran over Purcell! Second string saw a lot of play."

Again the season ended with a lopsided victory over the other new school, LaSalle. Brother Choquette recorded the start of a Moeller tradition that endured for more than 20 years.

The honoring of the first seniors went off very nicely. Dads were well pleased and very appreciative. Giving them a twelve-by-fourteen blue patch with their boy's number in gold sewn on the patch was quite unique. Several of the seniors should surely get college offers. (Eight did.) All-around wonderful boys, good coaching gave us a terrific season. We were heard of!!

After a routine 8–2 year in 1964, Moeller's first unbeaten season and first GCL championship followed in 1965. Roger Bacon, ranked third in Ohio, was shut out, 17–0. Sixth-ranked Dayton Chaminade, Gerry's alma mater, saw an unbeaten record ruined, 15–6. And Newport Catholic, rated third in Kentucky, was crushed, 39–6, in the last game of the season. Moeller finished 1965 ranked third in the state, and Tom Backhus, who would become one of Gerry's assistants at Notre Dame, was named Moeller's first high school All-American.

Gerry followed his first GCL title with 11 more in the next 15 years. His record for 18 seasons in the toughest league in the state is 92–11–1. He won 40 straight GCL games from 1972 through 1980, and eight league titles in a row. Three schools, Newport Catholic, McNicholas, and Purcell, whose enrollment had declined below 600 by 1980, eventually dropped out of the league in football, and the remaining schools became increasingly bitter about Moeller's dominance. A. J. Schaub, who became president of the GCL the year Moeller won its first league championship and announced his retirement soon after Gerry accepted the job at Notre Dame, had declared early in the 1980 season: "The league is ruined. We don't have the spirit we once had. The other schools know they're playing for second place in football."

The stature the Moeller football program achieved, and the national attention focused on Gerry and Moeller in later years, were in large measure the results of two developments of the 1970s—the inception of state football playoffs in Ohio and Gerry's so-called "high school super bowls" pitting Moeller against successful schools from other states. The computerized ratings that determine playoff participants in Ohio forced schools with serious playoff ambitions to improve their schedules, which in turn compelled many of them to play Moeller. Playing a broad intrastate schedule, with the state champion decided on the field instead of by polling coaches or sportswriters, allowed Moeller to establish its superiority without dispute. Playoffs provided an incentive and recognition. Building a reputation in state playoffs only made the out-of-state games more appealing, provided the visitors were making a name, too.

Moeller's program of national competition began innocently in 1977 with a game against Brother Farrell High of New York City. It was played at the University of Cincinnati's Nippert Stadium and attracted a crowd of 22,000—while the Reds and Atlanta Braves were playing before 19,653 in Riverfront Stadium, about three miles away. More significantly, the game was covered by the New

York *Daily News, Sports Illustrated,* and newspapers outside of Cincinnati.

Farrell High's head coach, a former University of Cincinnati player named Denny Barrett, proposed the game to Gerry in a phone call after hearing Gerry speak at a coaching clinic in Atlantic City. Farrell had won 27 games in a row and a couple of city championships, and Barrett had an open date to fill. Gerry didn't know what to say. His assistants urged him to accept the challenge. He told Barrett: "Okay, but you'll have to raise the money. I can't give you a guarantee." Moeller won easily, 30–0, but each school cleared more than $21,000.

With that kind of a payday, it seemed like a nice addition to Moeller tradition, so Gerry began scheduling at least one out-of-state opponent each year. A guarantee of at least $10,000 became part of the deal. Dallas Jesuit came and was conquered, 37–7, in 1978. The next year perennial Pennsylvania champion Penn Hills of Pittsburgh opened the season with a 30–13 loss to Moeller, then won nine straight. Three weeks later defending Michigan champion Detroit Brother Rice was a 33–14 loser to the Moeller machine.

"For the success he's had against those teams," cracked Ohio High School Athletic Association commissioner Richard Armstrong, "he could probably find competition just as good right here in Ohio." Aware of strong sentiment against Moeller's interstate spectacles among many Ohio school administrators, Armstrong nevertheless relished the success of an Ohio team against proven programs from such football-proud states as Pennsylvania and Texas. He even attended the Dallas Jesuit game.

Brother Eveslage, who returned to Purcell as principal in 1967 after Moeller's first two league championships, never thought anyone could accomplish what Gerry achieved in the GCL.

"I'd seen Massillon play Cathedral Latin in Cleveland," he said. "I'd seen high school football all over the state. I thought it would take a good coach just to compete in the GCL, just to keep his head above water. I hadn't the slightest inkling Gerry would be able to do all that he did."

Gerry's goals were modest enough in the beginning. "Looking back," he says, "we just wanted to build a solid football program, be competitive, and have the kids be proud to be a part of it."

THE END OF AN ERA

GAME THREE: MOELLER vs DeMATHA (Maryland)

September 13, 1980

When an out-of-state opponent came to Cincinnati to test Moeller, Gerry was publicity-promotion man first, athletic director and hospitality chairman second, and head football coach third.

Gerry the PR Man prepared for DeMatha by calling newspapers in Dayton, as well as in Cincinnati, to line up stories early in the week. "If a story is going to help the gate," he explained, "it has to run on a Monday or a Tuesday or a Wednesday. Stories on the day of a game don't sell many tickets." Conversely, TV time on game day can help. He made the rounds of local television stations, too, arranging for on-the-scene interviews with all three later in the week.

Gerry the Promoter asked a favor of Bob Trumpy and was invited to appear on the former Bengal tight end's sports talk show—an hour and 15 minutes to promote the big game on 50,000 watts, clear-channel radio. "We have to combat the Reds and Dodgers this weekend," he reminded. "They play Saturday night, too, and they're fighting for the pennant!" Even Football Faust knows Cincinnati is first and foremost a baseball town.

"Go see the Reds Friday night and Sunday," Gerry told Trumpy's listeners. "Saturday night, bring your radio down to Nippert Stadium and *listen* to the Reds while you *watch* Moeller and DeMatha."

Trumpy winced. "I'm not allowed to say that kind of thing on the radio," he whispered. The Reds' front office is rather sensitive to any overt suggestion to stay away from Riverfront Stadium, more so when it is broadcast on the flagship station of the Reds Radio Network.

Gerry the Athletic Director paid as much attention to weather forecasts and ticket sales updates as did Gerry the Coach to scouting reports and the game plan. "They're talking about possible thundershowers Saturday night," he frowned. "Ticket sales are starting to pick up, but we have a long way to go. We need good weather."

In the back of his mind was a worrisome thought: *Maybe the novelty of seeing Moeller cream an out-of-state opponent was wearing off by now!*

DeMatha High School is located in Hyattsville, Maryland, just over the state line from the District of Columbia. Nationally, De-Matha is better known as a basketball player's Moeller. Adrian Dantley, Sid Catlett, Kenny Carr, and Hawkeye Whitney—who achieved collegiate and professional stardom—all played their high school basketball at DeMatha, as did dozens of other familiar names. Basketball coach Morgan Wootten is a legend himself. The DeMatha football team, nevertheless, had won 19 games and lost only two in the two previous seasons, and the films showed two valuable assets. "They're big, and they have some very skilled athletes," observed Gerry the Coach.

In the "Travel League," DeMatha might just have ranked No. 1. Jerry Franks, DeMatha's head coach for nine years, has a vocabulary similar to Gerry Faust's. "We like to do things first class," he says. That is why, in 1976, he scheduled a game in California and followed it with an open date.

"We took the varsity and the jayvees, more than two hundred people altogether. We played the game, then stayed in California for a week! We saw San Francisco, Lake Tahoe, the state capital at Sacramento, Napa Valley—and then we flew down to Los Angeles and went to Disneyland and Beverly Hills! We spent thirty-three thousand dollars in one week!" Two years later, attempts to schedule a game in Florida fell through after the team had raised $16,000 with fruit sales and all-night bingo. "I said, 'Heck, we'll wait until spring and then take the whole team down there for a week's vacation and enjoy the warm weather.'"

DeMatha was playing as many as five out-of-state opponents each year under Franks. The all-boys school of 900 did not have a marching band, but its wind ensemble was rated best in the nation in 1979. The musicians had traveled, too—visiting Rome and Hollywood.

When the DeMatha traveling squad landed at Greater Cincinnati International Airport, players, parents, and coaches were greeted with Gerry's idea of red carpet treatment—a brass band and a police escort. Gerry and his four captains were planning to welcome everyone personally while the Moeller musicians played in the background, but a serious truck accident closed the interstate highway leading out of downtown Cincinnati. Gerry missed his own party. Streaking toward the airport more than an hour late, Gerry saw the motorcade pass him going in the opposite direction. He made a U-turn across the median, overtook the buses, and waved them to the shoulder. Then and there, on a rural stretch of expressway, he finally said, "Welcome." That night the visitors from Maryland were treated to a reception at their hotel.

"I can't believe this!" said one DeMatha mother. "They couldn't be any nicer."

This game was Moeller's third of the season but DeMatha's first, inviting pre-game analyses that reached conflicting conclusions. DeMatha will struggle with the usual season-opening jitters and mistakes; or, DeMatha has had two extra weeks to scout and prepare for Moeller, and thus will be ready for an upset. Moeller has had two games to get the bugs out and will be sharper; or, Moeller has had only five days to get ready for DeMatha and really does not know what to expect. Defensive line coach Steve Klonne, typically, studied films of DeMatha scrimmages until he no longer needed a projector to see the movies. "It's a question of how good their competition is," he decided. "They look like a good team, but I don't know if they play the caliber of teams you find around here." Gerry couldn't say. "I can't really judge a team if I haven't seen them in person, and I didn't get a chance to see DeMatha myself. I won't know until I see them on the field." Said DeMatha's Jerry Franks: "We figure this game will decide whether we're nine-and-one or ten-and-zero this season."

It had been a busy week at Moeller. Warner AMEX Cable Communications continued to seek a deal that would add Moeller football to its cable television program lineup, and former New York Giants head coach Allie Sherman was trotted out to make the latest pitch. But Gerry the Athletic Director was steadfast about terms Warner was reluctant to consider. "I can't afford to lose money on a deal like that," he said. "Putting those games on TV is bound to cut into our gate. We have to get enough out of a TV deal to make up for that, and then make it worthwhile." Gerry the PR Man kept busy escorting a delegation from *LIFE* magazine, the national media's representative for this game. Photographer Mike O'Brien shot more than 100 rolls of film in a week.

During pre-game activity, when the starting lineups are announced, the offense and defense walk through their formations, and the careful process of psyching up begins, Gerry the Coach sounded a familiar theme: Another "must" game . . . the toughest opponent yet this season . . . another team that can "make" its year by beating Moeller . . . every player must continue to improve . . . everyone must be ready to play harder than ever before . . .

"I know each week we ask you to give more and more," he said to the team. "And each week you have to give more and more because of the schedule we've got."

At Benediction in the chapel, senior halfback Tim King, who was baptized just before the season started, emphasized two important points to his teammates. "No out-of-state team has ever beaten Moeller," he said. "Remember! *They* called *us.*"

Eight-year-old Tommy Hergott was one of the week's special guests. Tommy was slightly more than three feet tall, paralyzed below the waist by the birth defect spina bifida. Gerry met Tommy after the 1979 season while speaking at the awards banquet of the Spartans, a youth football organization in neighboring Northern Kentucky. The Spartans were special to Moeller; they had exported seven members of the 1980 Moeller team.

"Gerry said he'd send Tommy a Moeller shirt and asked if he'd like to see a game next season," Tommy's father recalled. "I thought he'd forget about the invitation, like most coaches would, but I called at the start of the season and he remembered everything."

In the locker room the heat of shouted pep talks had reached its peak when Gerry turned and recognized the bright-eyed little boy with the permanent crutches.

"Tommy! Want to say something?"

There was a pause as the giants in body armor fell silent.

"Thank you," Tommy said softly.

Three members of the Ohio General Assembly gathered on the 50-yard line moments before the kickoff to officially welcome the DeMatha Stags to Cincinnati and Ohio. Skydivers were supposed to deliver the game ball to midfield, but winds aloft forced cancellation of the jump as their plane circled the stadium.

"Go out and have a good time," Coach Franks told each of his players as they filed down the walkway from the locker room to the field. "Have some fun tonight."

But Moeller was much too quick. It was 21–0 by halftime and DeMatha had not yet made a first down. Some fun. Two more touchdowns made a 34–0 final score. At Riverfront Stadium, meanwhile, 38,542 fans watched the Dodgers score twice in the ninth inning to beat the Reds for the second straight night, 3–2; Moeller-DeMatha had drawn about one fourth of that.

"The gate wasn't great, but it wasn't bad," Gerry the Athletic Director said wearily in the Moeller locker room an hour or so after the game. He had done some quick figuring in his head. "We'll each make about eleven thousand."

4

'Drill, Drill, Drill'

There was no great secret to the success of the Moeller football program under Gerry. The key was coaching. Gerry's assistants were professionals, and their football was sophisticated. The offense ran 35 plays from 12 formations; the offensive line could block five ways for each play. The four-four defense was developed and perfected at Moeller in the late 1960s, and when the assistant coach who conceived it left Moeller, he extracted from Gerry a promise to never share the fine points of the defense with anyone. Its effectiveness was well documented. In almost 6,000 rushing attempts, Moeller opponents gained barely more than two yards per carry. They averaged less than 10 points per game and scored three touchdowns or more only six times in 193 games.

Gerry concentrated more on the Moeller attack. His offense was imaginative, entertaining, and very aggressive. He liked traps, dives, draws, and the power sweep. He disdained rollouts, screens, and the quarterback option. He liked to throw 12 to 15 times a game—from the pocket—and could count on roughly 150 yards passing whenever Moeller threw that often. He could count on scoring, too. In those 193 varsity games he coached at Moeller, his quarterbacks threw 216 touchdown passes.

Though he is neither foolish nor reckless, Gerry is not afraid to take chances. He will throw when he ought to run; he'll throw long when he ought to throw short. He will fake a kick and run or throw whenever the opposition leaves itself vulnerable. He is such a quick study and so knowledgeable about the game of football that he can analyze opponents' strengths and weaknesses and anticipate with uncanny accuracy. He often said he could watch an opponent the first five minutes of a game and conclude which plays, defenses, and strategy would be most effective against that team. He will go for first down on fourth-and-short more often than most coaches. And faced with that difficult choice of one last play to win or tie, he will go for the victory. He always plays to win.

Despite his intense competitiveness, Gerry would never allow Moeller to be a win-at-all-costs football factory. There were no profane coaches brutalizing teenagers with boot camp abuse, teaching boys to hate and hurt the opposition. There were no chicken-wire pens on the Moeller practice field. Moeller football was technique and execution, strength, quickness, and finesse. "We hardly ever scrimmage because we don't want anybody injured in practice," Gerry told clinic groups. "All we do every day is drill. We just drill, drill, drill."

A typical midweek day of practice would begin with group meetings at 2:45 and end with timed laps at about 5:30. The group meetings would last 30 minutes: ends and backs would be throwing the ball; tackles, guards, and centers would be walking through blocking assignments; defensive backs would be reviewing coverages; and the rest of the defense would be watching films on the opposition offense. The next hour was devoted to drills. "The key to football is drilling," Gerry has said over and over. "Teaching the kids the special techniques is the name of the game."

Most coaches schedule specialties at either the beginning or end of practice because they do not involve the whole team. But Gerry set aside 20 minutes right in the middle of the daily workout to concentrate on kickoffs, punts, and placekicks. "If we have it before practice," he reasoned, "it is not important. If we have it at the end of practice, they think practice is over. We have the specialty period in the middle of practice, in the middle of the field. Two coaches help me; the others take the other players off to the side and work on techniques. We do not have anyone standing around."

Dummy drills against the sophomore offense and defense would consume the last 45 minutes to an hour: short yardage or goal-line defense for 10 minutes; pass defense and prevent defense for 15 minutes; then regular team defense for 20 to 35 minutes; short yardage offense—first-and-goal from every yard line inside the 10—for 10 minutes; the passing game for 15; and the running game for 20 to 35. Inflated or padded cushions absorbed most of the punishment in dummy drills, hence the name. Moeller practiced in full gear only twice a week, and even those days full contact was limited. "We found the kids performed better if they were not always hitting," Gerry said. "You must have them hungry to hit. We go dummy a lot, and by Friday they are ready to hit. If you hit every day, they don't have anything to look forward to on Friday night."

Moeller football players were not required to run wind sprints at any time during the season. Gerry used timed laps around a track one fifth of a mile long. Backs were required to run their first lap in 60 seconds, the second in 65, and the third in 70. Linemen's times were 70, 75, and 80. They received a one-minute break between laps, and anyone who failed to complete a lap in the prescribed time had to run another And if he was still too slow, another. "There were times when I would like to have come off the practice field and told the boys they didn't have to run their laps," Gerry confided. "But you do what is best for the kids. Those kids must be in shape or they'll get hurt. You'd be surprised how this got them in shape. They didn't want to run another lap, so they pushed themselves."

From freshman to varsity, the coaches at all levels of the Moeller program received the same instructions from Gerry. The directives filled a single mimeographed sheet distributed to all coaches at a staff meeting the day before the start of summer practice. "Things Expected Of A Football Coach At Moeller High" included:

Set a good example at all times to the students.

Strive to eliminate profanity and keep everything associated with football on the highest possible level.

Carry out your assigned responsibilities with enthusiasm.

Have an Active interest in football.

Be an authority on the game.

Devise, suggest, contribute.

Start practice on time. At Moeller Time is one of our greatest problems. Therefore, we must all give detailed attention to getting everyone dressed, organized, and started in the shortest possible time after school is over.

Be Aware of the Practice Schedule and Follow It.

Every minute on the field should be a critical one. Each coach has direct responsibility for different positions and phases of the game. On every play, every coach should be coaching, not conversing or day-dreaming or resting.

Be conscious of morale factors—keep the players hustling constantly.

Do not allow personality conflicts to interfere with your functioning as a coach.

Basically our job is to teach boys how to block, tackle, and move. We must accept every opportunity to improve upon these abilities.

You will always be provided with a copy of the practice schedule prior to practice. If you do not understand the details of every activity under your supervision, it is your duty to check with the head coach on your level.

If times are too long for your drill, change, improvise—be prepared to do something of value.

The Coaching Staff Is a Team in Itself . . . Do Your Part.

No member of a coaching staff ever has "free time" on the practice field. You should be observing, correcting, analyzing, evaluating, criticizing, complimenting, organizing, anticipating, adjusting, and learning constantly.

I Think We Have the Best Balanced Coaching Staff in the G.C.L. Let's Prove It to Everyone. Let's Have the Best Teams on All Three Levels.

The Best Way to Teach Is by Example. Let's Be Excellent Teachers.

The season was an endurance test for the coaches, stretching from mid-August to late November with almost no free time. Summer practice began at 8 in the morning and ended, for the coaches, after 6 o'clock. During the season there was practice Mondays through Thursdays after school, a game or scouting on Friday nights, a meeting with the varsity on Saturday mornings, often another scouting assignment on Saturday nights, and meetings of the coaching staff to plan for the coming week on Sundays. In addition, coaches were variously assigned to handle stadium operations or program sales on game nights, locker room sign-making on Sunday mornings, or supervision of a Saturday afternoon flag football league for third grade boys. Gerry usually sent out three teams of scouts each Friday night, flying coaches to out-of-town games in one of two private planes provided without charge by business acquaintances. On the busiest weekend of the 1980 season, Moeller coaches scouted four local games plus games in Canton, Ohio, and Hyattsville, Maryland. Speaking to business audiences, Gerry often points to the 1979 season, when the coaching staff worked 45 days in a row.

"I didn't even know it," he recalls. "One of my coaches told me, and I said, 'Geez Crickets! You guys get next Sunday off.'" But "half of them came in the next Sunday anyway, because they had work to do."

Seven coaches worked full time with the 76-man varsity; four were assigned to the sophomore team, which had between 50 and 55 players; and seven coaches, including four volunteers, handled a freshman group of 70 to 80 boys. The volunteer coaches for the most part were former Moeller players who passed up college football. "They worked for the experience," Gerry said, "whether they were planning to go into coaching or not. Whatever they did after they graduated from college, they were way ahead of everybody else because of the exposure, the experience of handling people."

Gerry drew up the practice schedule and made sure it was followed to the minute. He checked on every group and pulled the pieces together during team drills. But his assistants did most of the teaching and coaching. At the end of every practice and before every game, he called on each coach to say a few words to the team. Sometimes he would guide the comments, not so much to make the coaches say what he wanted to hear but rather to keep them from saying anything he did not want the players to hear. "Gotta keep it positive." He called all of the plays in games, but a few hours before kickoff he would ask each varsity coach to name his piece of the starting lineup. "They've been working more closely with the kids all week," he explained. "And they know what they want to try to do in the game. If I think they're making a mistake, I'll tell them they should make a change. But that doesn't happen very often. They know their personnel."

Knowing the personnel and placing players in the proper positions, Gerry emphasizes, is one of the secrets to high school coaching—especially high school coaching. Gerry was a master at it. Basically he would take the smaller, faster kids for defense and the bigger but slower kids for offense. Moeller defensive ends, for example, rarely weighed more than 180 pounds; defensive tackles rarely exceeded 200 pounds. Offensive tackles ranged from 220 to 260, and two guards and the center ranged from 200 to 220. "We can adjust our line splits offensively to the speed of the players," Gerry explained. "You can't do that on defense. If you have a big, fast kid, you can make the splits real wide. If you have a slow kid, you have to move the splits in."

Gerry used what he called the "three principle." In simplest terms, it meant he had one extra starter for each position, such as a third end, a third tackle, a second center . . . His first-team offense, then, included 18 players, the first-team defense, 17. He instituted the two-platoon system at Moeller on his first day, and by 1970 he had enough coaches to make it work on a collegiate or professional level. There were practice days at Moeller when as many as 14 separate groups of players were supervised individually.

"We can take a lesser athlete and, by training him for four years, make him as good one way, we feel, as if we played a star both ways," Gerry said. "When you work with a kid for two hours a day and you work with him at the same position all year long, he is going to be more knowledgeable. When you are more knowledge-able, you have more confidence. When you have more confidence, you are a better football player. If you don't know what you're doing, you will be hesitant, and if you hesitate you will get beat. You have fewer injuries with two-platoon football; the players have time to rest because they're not on the field all the time. Injuries come when players are fatigued."

Platooning provided Moeller with a definite tactical advantage, too. Coaches regularly called the entire offense or defense together on the sideline while the other unit was on the field. If Moeller's opponent did not platoon, the coaches had to make their ad-justments at halftime or juggle the lineup to get information into the game. There were even occasions when a Moeller coach assigned to watch the game from the press box and suggest strategy by telephone to the bench would come down to the field and conduct a sideline meeting with the offense or defense if a major adjustment was needed.

In the style of a successful corporate executive, Gerry sur-rounded himself with good people and left them alone. "Gerry is the first coach who has really let me coach," said defensive line coach Steve Klonne, who assisted at three other high schools before joining the Moeller staff in 1978. "He hires you to coach. If you can't do the job, he gets somebody else."

The molding of Moeller's state champions began with Jeff Leibert and Ted Hall. Most high schools give the freshmen to their newest, youngest, least experienced coaches. And, just as the players move through the program, those young coaches advance as quickly as openings arise. But between them, Leibert and Hall coached Moeller freshmen for 19 years under Gerry. "It's like running our own varsity program," Leibert said. "The only difference is you start every year with a bunch of kids who have to be taught everything." And just when they start looking like football players, Hall sighed, the season is over and they move on to the sophomore team. It was his one frustration after 11 years as a freshman coach.

Leibert was too small to play high school football, so he became a trainer at Louisville St. Xavier and the University of Kentucky. He was coaching grade school football in Cincinnati and working in computer systems at Procter & Gamble when Gerry hired him to be both a trainer and a coach.

Hall is a charter Man of Moeller, so to speak. He played on the first Moeller varsity, graduated in 1964, and returned as Moeller's sole freshman coach in 1970 after playing college ball at Iowa State. "Total chaos," he said of his early days alone with the freshmen. "Fantastic," he said of the five coaches eventually working with him and Leibert.

A freshman class of 285 boys at Moeller could be expected to produce about 120 football candidates. Leibert and Hall would cut that to the mid-seventies in the first two weeks, conferring with Gerry. They talked quickness, intensity, size, intelligence, grade school prowess, toughness, and, of course, potential. "There are about thirty-six players and maybe thirty-six others with potential in every freshman class," Hall said. Fully half of them were in the stands by their senior year.

Projecting the next four years of a 14-year-old's growth and development carried with it a certain finality in the case of Moeller's freshman football candidates. "In my eight years, we have never had a kid cut as a freshman come back and make the football team in later years," Leibert said in 1980. "It just doesn't happen. If they're not in our top seventy to begin with, they just don't have it. We don't make mistakes with these kids. We know what we're looking for, and we've got six or eight guys evaluating them and discussing them before we make the cuts." The process was a bit self-fulfilling, Leibert conceded. The boys learned so much in one year in the freshman program, that any boy who missed it could not make it up. He was too far behind. Another fact of life was rarely defied. "If you don't *play* as a freshman," Leibert added, "you won't play at Moeller." It was proven dramatically by the 1979 national champs. The starting offensive line was the freshman line of 1976, and eight defensive starters were freshmen regulars.

The Moeller tradition was perpetuated in many ways. Freshmen and sophomores, for example, dressed alongside upperclassmen so they would grow up with the mystique, excitement, pressure, discipline, and sacrifice that came with playing for a championship every week of the Moeller season. "The kids don't really have much fun until the junior and senior years," varsity offensive backfield coach Paul Smith, a former sophomore coach, observed. "As freshmen and sophomores they really work hard." The freshmen and sophomores were scheduled to play at night and out of town at least once during each season, if possible, to acquaint them with the varsity elements. The winning tradition permeated the whole program—no Moeller team lost a game at any level in either 1979 or 1980, a combined total 57 victories and 2 ties.

Leibert helped the indoctrination process with what he called his national championship drill for freshmen. They would come together in a huddle, jump up and down, hug each other and yell and holler—just the way they would act if they had won a national championship. Like any other drill at Moeller, this one was repeated until everyone did it perfectly. "You'll only get to use it once a year when you're juniors and seniors," Leibert would tell the boys, "so you gotta get it right the first time."

The "national championship drill" helped nervous 14-year-olds to relax and brought them together at a time when they still felt like strangers around each other. It also, obviously, propagated that winning attitude. "Kids, any people, will only do what they think they can do," Leibert reasoned. "You gotta tell them how to win. If you don't tell them about it, they won't know how it feels."

The six full-time varsity assistants on the 1980 staff shared 75 years of cumulative coaching experience. Paul Smith, who replaced a man with 16 years of service on the varsity staff when he took over the offensive backfield for the 1980 season, was the junior in experience, although he had been coaching for seven years. The offensive linemen were entrusted to Jim Higgins, a former pro lineman, and Pat Orloff, a former high school head coach—a knowledgeable combination. With Klonne on the defense were two fixtures at Moeller, secondary coach Mike Cameron, who worked with Gerry for 14 years, and linebacker coach Ted Bacigalupo, the defensive coordinator, who spent 12 seasons with Gerry.

Higgins played with Roger Staubach in high school and against him in the National Football League. Three years with the Edmonton Eskimos of the Canadian League and two years with the Miami Dolphins preceded his arrival at Moeller. He was called the best high school line coach in the country by everyone who watched him at work, and every offensive lineman who started for him in his seven years at Moeller received a college football scholarship. "If a kid starts in the offensive line for us, and he's over six feet tall and two hundred pounds," Gerry often said, "we can virtually guarantee him a scholarship." Higgins never stopped teaching, even on the field during games. He would grab a small chalkboard and call the offense around him literally every time the defense took the field. He did not want his offensive linemen wandering around the sideline when they were out of the game. He wanted to keep them thinking.

While Higgins was teaching technique on the field, Orloff was studying defenses from the press box. Some people would say he was overqualified to be an assistant coach, even at Moeller. An All-Mid-American Conference guard under Ara Parseghian and John Pont at Miami University in the late 1950s, Orloff coached for 20 years at two public schools, including two five-year tours as a head coach. Gerry chose him as an assistant coach in a high school all-star game in Cincinnati in 1975 and again in the game two years later. After that, Orloff decided he might as well work for Gerry full-time. "I wish I had done this a long time ago," he said three years after making the switch. "Being an assistant coach at Moeller is more enjoyable and more satisfying than the years I spent as a head coach." Pat continued to teach at a public school five miles from Moeller and took "personal days" to get away from classes whenever Moeller was playing, practicing, or traveling on a school day.

Higgins, Orloff, and Klonne also supervised the weight training program. Klonne, a dean's list student in college, won the Ohio State Powerlifting championship in the 242-pound class in 1971 and finished third in the Midwest. He was runner-up twice in the Mr. Cincinnati body-building contest while in college and lifted weights daily after practice. On a hard-working staff, Klonne was the resident workaholic. Usually the last to leave for home, he would replay game films until he had them virtually memorized. He is a perfectionist, and Gerry worried about his intensity. Once, after Moeller had beaten a tough opponent by three touchdowns, Steve fretted and moped about the two touchdowns the Moeller defense had allowed and the breakdowns that had resulted in some big plays. "Steve, you look like we just lost," Gerry growled outside the locker room where a noisy celebration was in progress. "C'mon. Let's see a smile." Klonne immediately produced an exaggerated, contorted smile. "That's not good enough," Gerry scolded. "You're not happy about this game, but you should be. Let me tell you, you have to learn how to enjoy a victory. It's fine to want to improve; it's fine to want to eliminate the mistakes; it's fine to want everyone to execute perfectly. But not everything is going to go just the way you want it. You have to realize that, and when you win, you have to enjoy it. You have to enjoy winning, and then go and try to correct the mistakes. If you can't enjoy winning, you shouldn't stay in coaching."

Ted Bacigalupo left Moeller once. He had been there six years when he quit to spend full time making money at the expense of bad golfers. Baci's business was retrieving golf balls from water hazards, reconditioning and reselling them at the rate of 4,000 to 6,000 balls a week in the summer months. The business went well, but he missed coaching. "The kids keep you young," he said. Baci returned to Moeller after only one season away, his business once again part-time. He is an astute, strong authority figure whose forceful, thoughtful halftime talks were second only to Gerry's. His 12 years at Moeller taught him how to handle the pressure. "I used to lose sleep the night before a game," he said, "but not anymore. I don't worry about playing the game. I work as hard as I can, and prepare the kids as well as I can. That's all you can do."

Mike Cameron came to Moeller straight from college. Gerry agreed to an interview at Mike's request, even though he had no intention of offering a job to someone without experience. Mike impressed Gerry so much in a short conversation, however, Gerry changed his mind. Mike became more than just an assistant coach. He was assistant athletic director, chairman of the physical education department and, as baseball coach, living proof that football was not the only sport that could prosper at Moeller. His baseball team won Moeller's first state championship in 1972—a year ahead of the football team's first playoff appearance. The pass defense Cameron coached was complicated. Seven different coverages had to be coordinated between the linebackers and the secondary. In 12 years the opposition completed only 35 of every 100 passes thrown against that defense. Cameron often asked himself about the scope of the Moeller football program; all the coaches on Gerry's staff did so at some time.

"I wonder, most of all," he said, "when I see our kids leaving school late in the season and it's already been dark out for two hours. But when the kids come back years later, when they visit school and talk about how much they miss it—that's when I know we're not doing the wrong thing. We ask an awful lot of our football players—weights the year-round, running all summer, ballet lessons for a lot of them, long practices, and a lot of preparation each week. But what we're really doing is giving them a chance, for maybe the only time in their lives, to say they were part of the *best* in something—*the very best.* And when it's all over, they have the satisfaction forever of knowing they reached inside themselves for everything they had, to excel, and succeeded."

Gerry always made it a point to remind his colleagues at coaching clinics that the game of high school football "is for the kids and not for yourself." Asked if he was getting tired of winning state championships after his fourth in five years, he answered: "If you are coaching for the kids, you'll never get tired of it."

From humble beginnings, Moeller became the best-dressed high school football team in America. Gerry designed the uniform himself, and Champion Sporting Goods decided to market part of it, the "Crusader" jersey. Moeller had warm-weather uniforms and cold-weather uniforms, natural grass shoes and artificial turf shoes, and the latest and best in protective equipment—down to pro-style gloves for offensive linemen at $30 a pair. Moeller's first-class weight room was the envy of most major colleges: it had more than 16,000 pounds of weights, space for 25 athletes to work out at the same time, and four qualified weightlifting coaches to individually tailor and supervise each boy's routine.

Despite Gerry's tendency to order everything in "extra large," the coaches could have modeled for magazine ads on game nights. Gerry provided a full wardrobe, from royal-blue double-knit slacks to cream-colored pullover sweaters. Managers and trainers had their outfits, equipment men, too. So did the man who filmed the games.

Even team doctors were provided windbreakers with "Moeller Team Physician" lettered on the front. "Any guy who works with us full time gets a coaching outfit," Gerry declared, "because they're important to the program." In all, it cost almost $5,000 just to dress everyone for a season.

"Our athletes are exposed to the best we can provide," he said, "the best coaching, the best equipment, the best training, and the best care. If I were a teacher only, I would want to expose my students to the best material possible, so they could get the most out of class. That's really all we do with the football program. There are many schools that can't do it on our level, and they're doing it to the best of their ability. For them, that's what high school football is all about. The kids have fun. They gain the same things our kids gain."

THE END OF AN ERA

GAME FOUR: MOELLER vs. TOLEDO WHITMER

September 19, 1980

A breather, at last. Although Whitmer had reached the state playoffs in 1979—losing to Moeller, 31–7, in the semifinals—graduation had not been kind to the Panthers. The term "rebuilding year" was never used at Moeller, but two losses in the first three games meant that was exactly what 1980 was destined to be for Whitmer. Accordingly, Gerry eased up on his troops. "You can't get them up *every* week," he said. "You have to give them a break whenever you can, with the schedule we play."

The buses were to leave for Toledo at noon, so the whole school was dismissed at 11; no sense penalizing the handful of teachers who do not coach football, or those few students who do not play the sport or march in the band. "We find we get more out of *all* the students the first four days of the week if they know *everyone* will be excused when the team leaves early on Friday," explained sagacious Father Krusling, the graying principal. "Of course, there's always some parents who want to know if they're getting everything they're paying for, so we allow for a day like this when we plan the year's schedule."

Before embarking, the team attended a 15-minute Mass, offered for a safe trip, and heard imaginative Father Putka, team chaplain, deliver a brief homily that somehow established a parallel between the sacrifice required to be a Moeller football player and the martyrdom of St. Januarius, whose feast was celebrated that day. Afterward, the boys packed their gear as a team, one item at a time as directed by "duffel bag" coaches. When the caravan hit the interstate highway, northbound, the first thing Gerry said was a rosary. Except for the Williford brothers, senior Rob and sophomore Steve, everyone forgot about the game for 198 miles. The Willifords, both flankers, had moved to Cincinnati nine years before, and the Whitmer game represented a homecoming. They would be playing before 19 aunts, uncles, and cousins.

"All the way up I kept telling myself it was no big deal," Rob said. "But the closer we got . . ."

A few players—defensive back size—crawled into the overhead luggage racks to snooze as the buses rolled past a succession of sleepy little towns: Troy, Piqua, Sidney, Anna, Botkins, Wapakoneta. In another era, when trains brought baseball fans to Cincinnati to see the "Redlegs" play, those towns made up a litany of excursion stops. But now they are just so many big green signs alongside expressway off-ramps. There was plenty of time for small talk, and Gerry chose his only hobby and his only vice—poker—as the topic of conversation.

Gerry plays poker the way he coaches football—to win—and enjoys the same degree of success. He plays once a week, except during football season; always quits at 11:30, whether he is winning or losing; and wins 90 percent of the time. "I play poker with a lot of coaches," he said, "and they all play poker the way they coach. A coach who's good at calling plays would be one who bluffs once in a while. A conservative coach would be one who always bids exactly what he's holding. I play poker against them just the way I coach football against them." Gerry learned his poker the same way he learned his football, at the right hand of his father. "Dad had a poker club once a month; I grew up watching." Over the years, Gerry developed his own approach to the game. "I scan the board," he said. "I watch the players' facial expressions. And I look for mannerisms. After playing with someone for awhile, I know their style." Playing poker, like playing football, "just requires self-discipline."

Amazingly, a few Whitmer fans had already taken their seats when Moeller arrived at the stadium more than two hours before kickoff. Either someone had forgotten to tell them that this game would be no contest, or Toledo residents merely wanted to get a good look at the legendary Crusaders. The game was a sellout, which meant that football fanatic Gus Morris of Ann Arbor, Michigan—who took a night off work and thus forfeited $100 in wages—had to pay scalper's prices to get a seat. For him, though, the trip would prove to be worth it.

Moeller dominated, as expected, but it was a sloppy performance. "Two hundred and twelve yards total offense and *only two touchdowns*," the Moeller coaching staff complained at halftime. Even worse was the report from Doc Kollman: linebacker Randy Barger spent the whole second quarter trying to remember where he was . . . defensive tackle Tim Dirr's shoulder will require rest . . . blue-chip offensive tackle Doug Williams has had his ankle stepped on and might have suffered a hairline fracture . . . and center Jeff Lytton is limping, too. It was just about the worst halftime injury report Dr. Paul Kollman had delivered in his five years as Moeller's self-appointed traveling team physician.

Doc Kollman, one of Gerry's poker-playing friends, joined the Moeller lineup after Gerry recruited his son, Paul Jr. "He wasn't an athlete," Doc hastily established. "He was a good student and he earned a one-year scholarship to St. Xavier and a four-year scholarship to Moeller. Since I had attended St. X, I naturally wanted him to go there, too. But, Gerry insisted that he go to Moeller." The doctor's son never played football, but he was a trainer for four years. "And now, he's a trainer in college," Doc Kollman said proudly. At Notre Dame, of course.

There were no more injuries in the second half, but Doc was busy. Steve Faust, the coach's 12-year-old son, could not breathe, a case of pleurisy. And then a member of the Moeller band showed up on the sideline on a stretcher, complaining of chest pains. On the field, Moeller continued to dominate. Rob Williford had scored in front of his relatives on a 14-yard pass in the second quarter, and midway into the fourth quarter a 25–0 lead meant little brother Steve could at least dirty his uniform, too. With less than four minutes to play, Gerry thoughtfully called for a pass to Steve: down the far sideline, look for the ball in the end zone. Reserve quarterback Tim Jolley's pass was perfect. It arched over the outstretched arms of the Whitmer defender, and Steve took it over the shoulder on the dead run. Touchdowns for both of the Williford boys! Final score: Moeller 32, Whitmer 0.

Gus Morris showed up in the Moeller locker room as Gerry tried to hurry everyone through postgame showers. Gus offered $50 for a Moeller jersey and was ignored. "How about a hundred?" Finally, Gerry ordered punter Jim Rohlfs to give Gus his gray Moeller T-shirt, free. "I'm going to hang it on the wall in my football room," Gus explained. "I've got jerseys and souvenirs from all the great football teams. And this is the finest high school football team I've ever seen."

The buses pulled away from Whitmer Stadium just before midnight. Again, Gerry started the trip with a rosary.

"Michael Hartman, Michael Hartmann"—one of Moeller's defensive captains, led the team in a cheer that required his mates to echo his every word. Hartmann's part went like this:

"When you're up, you're up . . .

"When you're down, you're down . . .

"And when you play Moeller . . .

"You're UPSIDEDOWN!"

Doug Williams rode home with his aching ankle, which later proved to be sprained instead of broken, immersed in a bucket of ice. Everyone else slept. The team arrived back at Moeller at 3:15 in the morning. No matter the hour, though, there were certain post-game locker room traditions to be observed. Gerry left school at 4 o'clock and went to a nearby hospital to check on his son, who had been X-rayed and was doing fine. Then he visited the Church of the Immaculata near downtown Cincinnati, to say some prayers in thanksgiving for a safe trip and successful game. It was 6 o'clock in the morning when his head at last touched the pillow it had left some 25 hours earlier.

Three hours later he was back at Moeller, preparing for the next week.

5

The Other Side of Moeller High

The least successful years in the history of the Moeller football program also happened to be the most difficult years in the history of the school. Between 1966 and 1968, Moeller endured 9 of those 19 exceptions to an otherwise perfect record in the first 18 years of varsity football: seven defeats and two ties. The young Crusaders won their second league championship in 1966, but lost three times, more than any other year. The worst licking of all came the following year, a 45–0 shellacking by still powerful Roger Bacon. In 1968 only six games ended victoriously. The struggle over changing social values that characterized the decade of the 1960s in America had spread to Moeller. This was the time of Vietnam: "Down with the establishment," and Woodstock: "Do your own thing."

It was all there in the Moeller microcosm when the Reverend Lawrence Krusling arrived in spring 1970. It was the era of the open campus and modular schedules—innovative education. Discipline had started slipping. Spirit was poor. The teaching staff had polarized into two camps, "the freaks and the jocks," as Father Krusling characterized them. Coaches seldom visited the faculty lounge, because few of them taught academic subjects, and teachers who did not coach were almost never seen in that club room known as the coaches' office. Students were caught in the middle of this social and educational conflict, and parents complained. The Marianists went to the archdiocese and asked for help—a priest from outside the order to provide leadership.

Father Lawrence Krusling had undergone delicate surgery in late 1969. It was a close call, a tumor in the colon. His doctor said there was only a 50–50 chance of beating it; more chilling still was the knowledge that Father Krusling had lost one brother to cancer and another to a heart attack. He had taken a leave from his parish in a poor neighborhood of Cincinnati and was convalescing at a relative's when the archbishop called and said, "How about getting back in education?" He had his choice of five jobs. The archbishop suggested Moeller. It gave this man of faith a big lift. He thought, "Gee, The Lord wants me around a little longer."

The situation that greeted Father Krusling was not easily or quickly reversed. He kept a diary of the struggle and termed the first three years "just plain hell." The first order of business was shaping up the discipline. That, obviously, involved more than just the student body. There was a philosophical difference among the staff that had to be resolved. In three years, half the faculty left. If the jocks did not win the battle outright, they at least contributed significantly to a broader victory. At the forefront of that triumph was a hybrid named Dick Barattieri, a muscular former college football player whose combined machismo and intellect destroyed the myth that a jock cannot possibly appreciate the arts and culture, too. With equal proficiency he coached the offensive line and taught Shakespeare, grammar, and poetry. His all-time hero was Odysseus, "an athlete who always used his head."

Barattieri taught six periods of English—no breaks, no study halls, no cafeteria duty—and would not be dissuaded from flunking deserving football players. He would arrive at Moeller at 5:30 in the morning to prepare for his classes. Before he moved up to the varsity, he coached the freshmen—just 135 beginners and him. Gerry burdened him with a scrimmage three days after equipment was issued, and scheduled the maximum 10 games.

"Do you want me to teach fundamentals or win ball games?" Barattieri asked.

"Both," Gerry replied.

Barattieri had made the most of his football scholarship at Xavier University, taking extra courses in philosophy, history, English, and political science. He proposed adding to the Moeller curriculum an advanced humanities program for seniors that would prepare them for the intense examination of societal differences they would confront through college study and life experience. He recommended combining the history of philosophy—the foundation of civilized thinking—with three related subjects: political science, man's attempt to apply a philosophy; literature, a people's attempt to express their philosophy; and history, the record of whether a philosophy succeeded or failed. Father Krusling approved. Some students were dubious the first time this jock taught a class in the new program, but the doubters were quickly convinced. At graduation that spring, the seniors asked Dick Barattieri to be their commencement speaker.

Barattieri left teaching and coaching in 1973 to become an insurance agent. It paid better. His place on the faculty and on the coaching staff was taken by Jim Higgins. They had grown up together, had played football at Purcell and Xavier together, had studied the same subjects in college together, and had shared an apartment—Higgins maintaining his half of the rent even during the six months he was gone playing pro football. As Moeller High headed into the 1980s, Barattieri's advanced humanities program had become one of the school's distinct academic specialties.

When Moeller's new principal was named in 1970, Gerry quickly placed a call to the athletic department of Middletown Fenwick, the last place Father Krusling had served as principal. "What kind of a guy is he? Does he like sports?" Gerry's reputation had preceded him with Krusling. "My only concern was, 'Is this guy sincere? If not, he doesn't have the respect of the kids.' " They met in short order, and when Gerry left, Father Krusling thought, "Thank God. There's a guy who's got some zip and go about him."

It was Father Lawrence Krusling—not Gerry Faust—who ran Moeller High School during an eight-year period in which the football team won 90 games and lost only three. The principal always retained the final word on anything involving the athletic department, and occasionally restrained his exuberant friend. Most of the time he encouraged Gerry and supported his efforts.

"He's one of a thousand," Father said. "He'll work twenty-four hours a day; he loves what he's doing. He's always a couple steps ahead of everyone else, and he gets criticized by people who would love to do the things he does but won't because he thought of it first. It would have been sinful for me to have put the wraps on a guy like that."

Eleven years as the principal at Fenwick, a very small coeducational school, convinced Father Krusling of the value of athletics in education. Fenwick was constantly overshadowed by the huge public school, Middletown High. The Middies especially had great tradition in basketball. The heralded Jerry Lucas, later an Ohio State All-American and National Basketball Association All-Star, led them to three state championships during his career alone. Football was not the same. "Fenwick had a chance to get in there in football, to get a little recognition," Father Krusling said. With his blessing Fenwick became the perennial champion of a league full of public schools three or four times its size. A few years after he left Fenwick, when football playoffs were introduced in Ohio, the Fenwick Falcons won a pair of state championships in their division.

"Football starts the year off. It sets the tone," Father Krusling said in an echo of Moeller's first principal. Football in the Moeller magnitude also spreads the school's academic reputation, he believes. "I can't get some of the principals to realize: Anytime these college coaches come to recruit our football players, they have to report back to their director of admissions. And we have so many recruiters visit our school. When one of our students applies to a school, they already know about us. They know all about our academics."

The Moeller alphabet was not limited to two letters, X and O. The three Rs did not stand for Running, Receiving, and Repeating as state champs. "The word is, if you're a big jock, go to Moeller. But if you're a student, go somewhere else," Father Krusling said with unholy sarcasm. "People are amazed to find out we have a forensic team that's in the finals every year, a chess team that's city champ, and a bunch of winners on *It's Academic* (a local television quiz show for high school students).

Moeller is respected academically by the admissions offices of some of the nation's best colleges and universities—Columbia, Stanford, Duke, Notre Dame, Harvard, Southern California, Northeastern. Admissions officers agree that Moeller students are well prepared for college study. They frequently compliment the school on the ability of its graduates to relate to college instructors, their scholastic habits, their willingness to help others, and their school spirit. On a 100-point scale, a minimum C grade at Moeller is a 75, and 70 is the lowest passing grade. College placement test scores are considerably above the national average, and almost 90 percent of each year's graduates enter college. About 10 percent of each graduating class obtains academic scholarships.

"We've always had a rivalry between the guidance department and the athletic department," said Brother Robert Flaherty, director of guidance, "to see if we could match them in the number of scholarships. The hard part for us is getting kids to take the time to fill out all the paperwork involved in applying for an academic scholarship."

A breezier picture of Moeller academics comes from one of Gerry's eighth grade orientation sessions:

". . . We have all the courses of study, the general course and the college prep course . . . and you can get in advanced placement if you're real smart; that's based on test scores . . . and we have a transitional program, if you're having trouble with reading or math or English when you get here. . . . You can take TV, where you can produce and direct and make TV programs . . . and there's film appreciation; it's a super course but it's tough. . . . We have foreign languages, French, German, Spanish, and Latin . . . and there's drafting and computer science. We have a great art program, too. Brother Wanda has his master's degree from Pratt Institute. You have to take a test to get into the art program. . . . We've got a super band; it's improved over the years. I think we're overtaking Bacon as the best band in the GCL . . . . We have a forensic club . . . and a photography club . . . and an electronics club—boy, those kids are whizzes—and a magic club—even a table games club. . . . We've had the number one chess team in the city three years in a row. . . . And we also have athletics; I think you've heard of our athletic program . . .?"

There was a definite kinship between academics and athletics at Moeller under Father Krusling's direction. Almost a third of the faculty coached football, and half of the teachers coached something. "A coach is more bound to the school," Father Krusling contended. "He's a better disciplinarian. He's closer to the kids." Moeller had so many coaches, he said, "because we analyzed our needs. Every time we had a teaching vacancy to fill, I went to Gerry and asked him if he needed another coach in any sport. If he could find someone in the right teaching field who also was a coach in the sport where we needed more help, and if that teacher met our standards and qualifications, he got the job over an equally qualified teacher who didn't coach."

Of the football staff, offensive line coach Jim Higgins taught theology, church history, and English literature; defensive line coach

Steve Klonne taught consumer economics; freshmen coach Jeff Leibert taught computer science. Coaches were also placement counselors, physical education instructors, and teachers in sociology, physical science, and business. Varsity soccer coach Jim Bauer was the head of the business department.

Father Krusling heard the jive about Gerry running the school. "If I were worried about getting recognition," he responded, "that would probably bother me. Gerry knew who was in charge. He had the basic respect for authority. To be a good boss, you have to take orders yourself."

Except for Fuzzy Faust, there is probably not another man Gerry respects or reveres more than Father Krusling. "He's a great boss, and a great priest, and a great educator; he loves kids. There was no question who runs Moeller High School. He does. Everyone who works for him knows that."

For the most part, the Moeller faculty was solidly behind Gerry, the football team, and the athletic program in general, though few expressed that support as openly and as graphically as Dan Ledford, Bill Braun, and Brother Charles Wanda. They staged some of the most elaborate high school pep rallies in America. Gerry was his own rally coordinator during the late 1960s. Staging pep rallies proved to be one of the few talents he lacks.

"They were terrible," he admits. "The kids didn't even want to go to them; they used to sneak out the doors and we had to put teachers at all the exits to make sure the students stayed. So I fired myself—I fired myself real quick and got smart."

Gerry asked himself who could put on the best pep rallies, and he answered: "The art teacher and the drama teacher." Brother Wanda and Dan Ledford began producing epic pep rallies, and students began jockeying for seats. Word spread and parents started attending them. They were Hollywood, Broadway, and NFL Films all rolled into one. "Those two are the most creative men I've ever met," Gerry said.

Brother Charles Wanda did not realize his vocation as early as the others in the Marianist community at Moeller, most of whom entered religious life directly from high school. Charlie Wanda graduated from high school in 1954 and went to work in the lamp division at General Electric in Cleveland, his hometown, and then enrolled at the University of Dayton. He graduated in 1959 with a bachelor's degree in art education and a commission in the Army

Reserves. Active duty included a tour at Fort Knox. He taught high school in Cleveland for two years. He entered the Society of Mary in 1962 and was assigned to Moeller in 1964. Summer course work led to a master's degree from the prestigious Pratt Institute in Brooklyn.

Dan Ledford was one of Brother Wanda's early students at Moeller. He studied radio and communication arts at Xavier University. A local theater background was an asset when he accepted a job teaching English and drama at his alma mater. Seven years later he moved up to become assistant principal and dean of students.

The arrangement with Gerry was very simple. "Gerry leaves it up to us," Dan said. "Whatever we need, we go get it and charge it to the athletic department." The results were truly phenomenal—intricate lighting, special effects, skits with clever dialogue, dance routines, films, sound and slide shows, huge dry ice exhibits. Very colorful. Very exciting. Very expensive. And very time consuming. They thought nothing of working until midnight for a week to prepare for one 10-minute segment of a pep rally.

As a school administrator Dan Ledford had no difficulty justifying the extravagance of the pep rallies he helped create. "What we are trying to say to the student body is, 'You have all the advantages. You have everything going for you. You have a good home, a good school, people who care about you. But it didn't just happen. All of this has been won by incredibly hard work, by the football team, by each student, by the faculty, by your parents. All kinds of work has gone into this. Enjoy it. Celebrate it. But realize what you've got and what it took to get it.' Our rallies are the place where the kids experience the oneness of what we all share."

The shows added a dimension when another Moeller graduate, Bill Braun, returned as a faculty member in 1977. Bill was salutatorian of the Class of 1972. At Xavier University he was a thespian of note—president of the XU Players, most valuable member of the organization, best actor, best technician. He went into television production at Cincinnati's WLW-T, a leader in live, local programming. A year later he brought his talents to Moeller, and it just may be that some of his rallies attracted more viewers than some of his television shows.

"It's the most unbelievable thing you'd ever want to see," Gerry would tell audiences everywhere he went. "We have over two thousand people at our rallies, and our enrollment is only a thousand! The place is jammed, all because these men are so creative.''

There was a time when Moeller's other athletic teams were poor second cousins to football in the Moeller athletic family. But that began changing shortly after Father Krusling became principal, partly at his gentle, but firm, insistence and partly because Gerry grew weary of the irritating criticism from outsiders that he was an athletic director who cared only about football.

"We needed better balance in the athletic department," Father Krusling said. "We were criticized validly because other sports didn't get the attention they deserved. I talked to Gerry about it. My feeling was, 'They're all Moeller students; they're entitled to this attention, and they're going to get it.' ''

By 1980 Gerry could point to a number of improvements and distinctions in the rest of the athletic program. Moeller was the only school in Ohio with its own indoor tennis courts; the track team had an indoor track on campus; the wrestling team had its own arena—all in the school's new athletic facility. Water polo was added as a varsity sport to strengthen the swimming program; Moeller was the only school in the GCL to have a freshman baseball team;and more than 200 boys were participating in track. Schedules were being upgraded and teams in several sports were beginning to travel, as the football team had been doing for years. The one goal Gerry wanted but failed to achieve was winning an award presented annually to the all-sports champion of the GCL as determined by final standings in all league sports. It would have been his vindication.

Gerry cooperated in every way—as long as it did not jeopardize continued success in football. Wrestlers were welcome to use the weight room as long as their workouts were scheduled around the football team's. When sports seasons overlapped, the basketball team should be out of the locker room when the football team began preparing on game night.

"I can't let anything hurt the football program, because it brings in the money for the whole athletic department," he said. "If we hurt football, we're out of luck money-wise." By order of the archdiocese, the athletic programs in all Catholic high schools must be self-supporting. No tuition or fee money may be used to pay any athletic expenses, including coaches' stipends or even utility bills for the locker rooms. "We can't go to the parishes for help,"

Father Krusling said. "They're all in debt. We can't go to the people. They have to pay tuition. Football pays the bills."

Around the GCL the belief was that Moeller lived too well. Its football budget alone was larger than most schools' entire athletic budgets. It was assumed that the school had to have faults that were obscured by football's tremendous success. The team of Krusling and Faust became an unpopular one.

"Everyone's attitude," said Father Krusling, was "'You gotta be doing something wrong. Nobody can keep a program like that going without doing something wrong.'"

THE END OF AN ERA

GAME FIVE: MOELLER vs. LaSALLE

September 26, 1980

Cecil B. DeMille would have been impressed with the spectacle. Woody Allen would have loved the characterizations. Neil Simon would have applauded the script. And Gene Kelly would have cheered the choreography. It was not Moeller's senior play, because Moeller does not have a senior play. What it was, simply, was Moeller's first serious pep rally of the football season, the usual noise, cheering, and fiery oratory, highlighted by some great special effects and a clever four-minute skit—"The Damnation of Faust." The show, as usual, was produced by Bill Braun and Brother Wanda and written, directed, and choreographed by Dan Ledford. They worked in the gym until midnight every night for a week, building the set and rehearsing the act. About 20 teachers, students, and volunteers put in 60 man-hours. The cost for this pep rally: $1,000.

The din created by a 90-piece band and more than 700 shouting, whistling, foot-stomping students had reached its peak when Dan, speaking as assistant principal, stepped to the microphone and called for quiet. "We're not here just to honor the football team today," he began. "We're here to celebrate Moeller High School as much as Moeller football. We're here to celebrate the band. . . . We're here to celebrate the senior class. . . . We're here to celebrate all the kids who sold so many festival tickets. We're here . . . to celebrate that we're all part of the *best, by-God high school* in America!"

The house lights dimmed, then went out. It was show time.

As the curtain opened, there, on stage, was Coach Gerry Faust at the blackboard, diagramming plays for the LaSalle game. Even though the actor was young and blond, everyone recognized the character immediately. It was those baggy shorts, the socks down around the ankles, the worn gym shoes, and, of course, that wrinkled blue shirt, hanging loose, with the words "Moeller Coach" across the chest. Out of nowhere appeared the other character in this little comedy. He was dressed in scarlet, had a tail and horns, and carried a pitchfork. He got Coach Faust's attention with a jab in the back pocket. Yes, the Devil had come to tempt Gerry Faust.

"Ah, Faust! For years I've tried to entice you into throwing a football game, but I've never succeeded. But now! Now, I have the weapon that's sure to get you!"

"Geez Crickets! I thought I told you I'm not interested in anything you have to offer."

"True, true, Faust . . . I've offered you *fame,* but *you* weren't interested . . . I've offered you *money,* but *you* weren't interested . . . I've offered you *sex,* but *no one else* was interested . . ."

"Look, Devil," Faust said firmly but politely. He never wants to hurt anyone's feelings. "I think you're a *super* guy, and I think you do a *super* job. But there's *nothing* you can offer me that could make me want to throw *any* football game, *much less* the *LaSalle* game."

Fiendishly, the Devil smiled.

"Oh, no?"

"NO!"

But then, suddenly, a band began playing faintly in the distance. It was a march . . . a fight song . . . "Cheer, cheer for old Notre Dame . . ."

"Hear *that?!*" the Devil leered.

"Oh, no!" Faust quivered. "Not the Notre Dame job!"

"You got it, Fuzz Ball! You lose this LaSalle football game and I'll see that you get the Notre Dame job you want so badly."

Faust pleaded with the Devil to relent, but Satan only moved in for the kill. As the Notre Dame fight song grew louder and louder, he began to dance, a little soft shoe at first. Faust watched pensively, and slowly was drawn into the dance. The pace picked up and they became a dazzling duet, performing several spirited routines before finishing with a polka. The dancing was almost enough to lure Faust into a deal with the Devil. As the music ended, Faust was on the Devil's knee. But then he jumped up, shoved Satan to the ground, and launched into a typically hoarse, typically fierce pep talk, directed at the Devil but intended for the student body.

"I'm not going to make any deal with you, Devil!" he began, his delivery gaining speed and intensity with each sentence. "I'm going out there tonight and give *a hundred and twenty percent!!* And the students are going out there *and give a hundred and twenty percent!!!* Everybody's going out there and give a hundred and twenty percent, because that's what it will take to beat LaSalle!!!!"

Background music at this point was from the opera. It was *The Damnation of Faust,* and the crowd was going wild. Gerry Faust himself could not have said it better. But the show was not over. Again the house lights went out. One at a time, the names of the 10 opponents on the Moeller schedule were illuminated in two-foot letters on a signboard two stories high. When all of the names appeared in blue light, the first four, already conquered, changed one by one to red. Then LaSalle was switched from blue to flashing yellow. Two Moeller seniors, electronics geniuses, designed and built the intricate switching system that controlled the lighting. They had spent their last few summers doing the same kind of work at the Kings Island Amusement Park, near Moeller.

"The rallies get better as the season goes on," Dan Ledford assured. "*God* will visit Gerry next week."

Based on past performance, it would have taken an act of God or a deal with the Devil for Moeller to lose to LaSalle. Seventeen years after the two schools began playing each other, LaSalle was still looking for its first victory over Moeller. There were some close games: 13–6 in 1964, 6–0 in 1966, 11–7 in 1973, and 10–7 in 1975. But always, Moeller prevailed. Of course, LaSalle was not alone in its need for supernatural assistance against Moeller.

LaSalle athletic director Bob Krueger, who started the LaSalle football program but got out of coaching after only a few years, was speaking for all league schools when he said in a newspaper interview the day of the game: "Throughout the years, the pendulum swung back and forth. Purcell was strong, then Roger Bacon; and Elder was always in there. Now it's a shame. Everyone's fighting for second place. It's a shame kids have to feel this way."

Gerry, of course, disagreed. He said so in the locker room just before kickoff. "You know what that means," he shouted to his players. "That means it's okay for Bacon to win; it's okay for Elder to win; it's okay for LaSalle to win—but it's not okay for Moeller to win! They're not going to take it away from us!"

LaSalle's seniors had beaten Moeller's seniors twice while growing up, 18−14 as freshmen and 14−0 as sophomores. This unquestionably was the game they had waited four years to play. But LaSalle assistant coach Ken Barlag, a 1967 LaSalle alumnus, knew firsthand how much a Moeller class improves with age. He and his classmates had beaten Moeller as freshmen and sophomores only to lose 6–0 as seniors. The 1980 game would prove to be no different.

LaSalle stopped Moeller inside the 10-yard line once in each quarter and at halftime it was a scoreless tie. Moeller finally scratched out a 2–0 lead on a safety early in the third period. A touchdown pass, a two-point conversion, and a fourth quarter field goal added up to a difficult 13–0 victory. The game ball could have gone to any of several Moeller players. Fullback Mark Brooks, one of the preseason All-Americans, had his first outstanding game. Punter Jim Rohlfs set up the safety with a spectacular kick. It was end Pat Keneavy who got Moeller on the board with a crushing end zone tackle. Little Tim King made Gerry's decision to go for a two-point conversion succeed by adjusting his pass route in midplay. And defensive back Rob Brown stopped LaSalle's best drive with a pass interception.

None of them, however, was honored with the game ball. It went, instead, to mentally handicapped Scottie, the only guy on the Moeller sideline wearing a LaSalle jacket. Scottie had a brother attending LaSalle, but Scottie was a Moeller fan, and his dream was always to stand on the Moeller sideline and watch the team play. Gerry, of course, went him one better. Seeing that red LaSalle jacket on Moeller's side of the field was the inspirational difference in a very tough game, Gerry decided. For that, Scottie deserved the game ball. He was presented with it in the center of the Moeller locker room.

"You made a dream come true for a boy who loves the game of football but can never play," Scottie's mother told Gerry. Scottie went home that night and took his football to bed with him.

6

How Big Is Too Big?

Like politics and religion, Gerry Faust and Moeller football were, above all else, debatable. The fundamental issue was the purely philosophical question of proportion: When does a high school program cease to be a high school program? And when one program becomes so advanced, so organized, and so dominant that competitive balance is destroyed, must the successful program be penalized into parity and its architect condemned; or must the competition make a similar commitment and work twice as hard to overcome? It is not a new question. Armed nations face it. Bankers, businessmen, and merchants face it. Even college recruiters face it. It is the competitive curse of human nature and the free enterprise system.

The many people who criticized Gerry and objected to the Moeller program were divided into two categories. There were those who did not really know him or understand the principles in question, or who were not big enough to even concede him points for obvious hard work and dedication. They reacted with predictable jealousy, animosity, and distrust. Ignorant of the facts or missing the point, they ripped him personally, publicly, and unfairly. And then there were the reasonable people. They respected Gerry for his ability, enthusiasm, hard work, and success. They never said he did not earn what he achieved, only that he was achieving it on the wrong level. That is not to say their honest differences of opinion did not produce some intense feelings. It was possible to admire

Gerry's genius yet roundly condemn the way he applied it and the results it produced. And many people did just that. They asked: Is it high school football when a team never loses? Is it high school football when a team is so well prepared for a game—because it has so many coaches—that even exceptional opponents are unable to succeed with even their most sophisticated plays? Is it high school football when a team plays opponents from across the nation? Is it high school football when a team is invited to play in a foreign country?

The ultimate extreme, an international game, arose early in 1980 when Moeller was invited to play in Tokyo that September against Rancho Cordova High School of Sacramento, California. It was to have been a sequel to the 1979 college game between Notre Dame and the University of Miami. It never had a chance. Citing an Ohio High School Athletic Association rule prohibiting travel beyond 300 miles for an athletic contest, commissioner George Bates, who was only weeks away from retirement, refused to sanction the trip. Ohio Governor James A. Rhodes interceded publicly by announcing a trade mission to Japan to coincide with Moeller's visit. The line of scrimmage had been drawn.

Throwback politician that he is, the governor chose just the right words to allow his message to fit between the lines. "Many of the industrialists who want to do business in Ohio will be attending the game," he said, "so I'm putting together a trade mission so it can accompany the Moeller football team and meet with Japanese businessmen during the trip. The Japanese are crazy about football." Noting that Rancho Cordova already had permission to make the trip, Rhodes added: "Ohio's image in Japan will be damaged if permission cannot be obtained for Moeller players to make the trip." He was not finished. "Just as every Ohioan was proud to see our All-Ohio Youth Choir leading the Rose Bowl parade, our citizens will be proud of the fine young people at Moeller. Additionally, I am sure you agree that the educational benefits these players will gain from the trip are a once-in-a-lifetime opportunity."

But Jack Schmidt, president of the OHSAA board of control, disagreed. And it was his board that would affirm or overrule the decision by George Bates. "I have to question the cancellation of school for one thousand kids so eighty kids can go to Japan to play football," he responded. Then he got to the heart of the matter: "The direction of how the Moeller program is going doesn't appeal to administrators throughout the state." The OHSAA remained steadfast. "I don't see how we can support the trip regardless of whether the governor supports it or not," Schmidt said.

Political pressure was really nothing new at the OHSAA. "Every time we have a rule someone doesn't like," Bates said, "the first person we hear from is the politician who represents those people. They say, 'They're my constituents.' But they mean, 'They might vote for me if I stick my nose into this.' "

Sources in the governor's office said Rhodes was ready to initiate action to put the OHSAA out of business as an independent organization by legislating the supervision of interscholastic athletics into the state department of education. But one day before Schmidt was to convene the board of control to formally reject Moeller's request for a travel rule exception, Gerry withdrew it and announced the school would accept the state association's decision. "We would have gone," Gerry said. He was quite certain. "The governor was going to force the issue, and there's no one who's going to buck the governor." Bates, though, was equally certain the OHSAA would not have yielded to political pressure. "I wouldn't have cared if the governor advocated it or not," he said. "My decision would have been the same. I think the governor can have his trade missions without a high school football team. It was just another approach to get support for Moeller's position." Moeller backed off for only one reason, Gerry said. "We didn't want to be the school that forced a battle between the governor and the board. I'm not saying that would necessarily be bad; we just didn't want to be the school that caused it."

The conflict raised some interesting issues that were never fully debated. If high schools should broaden a teenager's horizons and prepare him for adulthood, for example, then how would a trip to Japan be bad? "There might be some validity to that argument," Bates conceded months after the issue was settled. "But it would be pretty hard to convince eight hundred and thirty-three other principals that because Moeller happened to have a football program of national acclaim, it should be allowed to play an international game in Tokyo or wherever. It's hard to justify that exception for one school."

Classes would not have been cancelled for 1,000 kids, as Schmidt contended in responding to the governor. Rather, Gerry said, the school calendar had been rearranged so that no student would have missed any class time. Moeller would have completed the trip in four days, which in itself left the man who succeeded

Bates as commissioner, Richard Armstrong, with a question:

"If you're going for the sole purpose of an interscholastic contest, if you're just going over and play the game and come back, how can you have time for that wonderful educational experience? If a good athlete knows he might go to Japan if he goes to a certain school, he will want his family to move into that school district. That's where the fair competition rule comes in. All schools should have the same opportunity to be competitive, and that doesn't hold true, for whatever reasons."

Gerry raised another interesting point regarding the OHSAA decision. At the time of the great Japan debate, another school in the state was preparing a group of students for a trip abroad. The students were musicians, and the school was Massillon—once the foremost high school football name in America but by 1980 over-shadowed, in Ohio and the nation, by Moeller. "They raised eighty-eight thousand dollars to send their band to Great Britain for two weeks," Gerry told anyone who would listen. "It makes you wonder why another school function that's not under the state athletic association can do a thing like that, but a football team can't make a similar trip."

George Bates: "In my opinion, Gerry was grasping at a straw to justify what he advocated for his program. Just because Massillon does it, does that make it desirable for all schools? I don't think the purpose of a high school program is to develop national or interna-tional competition—in anything. The vast majority of colleges don't even do those things. You have to leave some of these things for adulthood."

Richard Armstrong: "We are not an activities association. We do not concern ourselves with anything but interscholastic athletics. I'm not so sure, personally, that it's so great for that band to go to Great Britain. If it's that good, let them play right here in Ohio for our old people."

Moeller football was the root of controversy within OHSAA on other fronts, too. The school's domination of the state football playoffs was a contributing factor in an attempt by some northern Ohio schools to exclude private and parochial schools from state tournament competition. The proposal was to create a separate division for them within the OHSAA. All member schools were eligible to vote in the referendum, and the proposal was defeated overwhelmingly in 1979. But another amendment to the state association's rules, inspired at least in part by Moeller's drawing power, was adopted and survived a court challenge. Under that one, no out-of-state student attending an Ohio school, whether public or private, is eligible for any interscholastic sport. Moeller had eight football players from nearby Northern Kentucky, two of them starters, at the time the rule was upheld in court. Their eligibility was not affected.

The popular assumption regarding Moeller's players from Northern Kentucky was that Gerry ruthlessly enticed them to come play for him. In fact, the first two Kentuckians who showed up on the Moeller football team were there because the parents of the boys had visions of their sons starring for the greatest high school team ever. They contacted Gerry. The boys contributed substantially, but they were not starters. Gerry made some speaking appearances in Northern Kentucky, as he did throughout the Greater Cincinnati area. If Fortune 500 companies sought him as a speaker, the demand among local youth organizations was even greater. Gerry accepted as many as he could. He spoke of values and principles, the things he believed in, and used Moeller football as his illustration. Given his innate ability to communicate with enthusiasm, and his absolute belief in what he was doing, his speeches had the effect of a recruiting pitch for Moeller football. Naturally, some of the better football players in his Northern Kentucky audiences liked what they heard and followed the lead of those first two interlopers.

In one sense, Gerry did recruit. He visited every parish grade school in the Moeller district and knew every promising athlete by his first name. He spoke at their banquets and attended some of their grade school games. He conducted all of Moeller's eighth grade orientation sessions, explaining the total academic and extracurricular program at Moeller to every prospective freshman. He did not emphasize football in these formal presentations, though at times he did a little extra talking to a football prospect individually if the boy still was undecided about attending Moeller. He promoted his school in many ways, with equal enthusiasm.

Only 6 of Moeller's 14 parishes sponsored grade school football teams, and two parishes did not have their own grade schools. Athletes in parishes without football teams participated in other youth football programs, and those without parish grade schools attended public elementary schools. Gerry went after Catholic boys in those situations with vigor, encouraging them to attend Moeller for the dual benefits of Moeller football and a Catholic education. Without fail, every time he approached a Catholic boy outside the framework of parish football or eighth grade orientation, someone interpreted it as cheating.

Gerry won the active support of the grade school principals, who urged their students to attend Moeller. One nun even asked his help when it appeared dwindling enrollment would force the elimination of football at her school. Gerry found another parish school facing the same problem and helped the two sisters set up a combined football team with boys from both schools. He organized a flag football league for third- and fourth-grade boys from all 14 parishes and assigned coaches from his staff to help run it, because "we want the boys in our district thinking Moeller football as early as possible." And he operated his own summer sports camp at Moeller to introduce boys to the atmosphere of Moeller athletics, attracting more than 200 boys for each two-week session.

But as George Bates of the OHSAA observed, the success of Gerry's football program was the best recruiter he had, and the only one he needed. That is why, when one businessman being transferred from Columbus to Cincinnati went house hunting late in the 1980 season, he began by visiting the Moeller athletic department. His burr-headed son stood six feet four inches tall, weighed 220 muscular pounds, and was still growing. The man wanted to know more about the Moeller program he already had heard so much about. And he wanted to know the communities within the Moeller district.

There were many players of suspicious origins on the Moeller roster over the years, but always there were plausible explanations. The classic case was a tailback with the Heisman Trophy name of Hiawatha Francisco, who was running "four-five forties" when he arrived as a freshman in 1979. Hiawatha's mother rented a house from Gerry, and, inevitably, the player-coach-landlord relationship made headlines. The Franciscos had been living in a neighborhood that was cleared to make way for an industrial park. Mrs. Francisco called Gerry and asked if he could refer her to a real estate agent who could help her find a house in the Moeller district. Her son's idol was Tony Hunter, the Moeller All-American who started breaking Notre Dame pass receiving records in his freshman year. Hiawatha wanted to be a star at Moeller, then play for Notre Dame, too.

Gerry told Mrs. Francisco he thought he was allowed to help her, but first he called the OHSAA to be sure. Then he provided the names of two friends, one his barber and business partner, Morris Roberts, who sold real estate as a sideline. Gerry and Roberts owned three houses as investments, and Roberts eventually showed one of them to Mrs. Francisco. Subsequently it was suggested Gerry had acquired the property just so he would have a place to offer the family of an outstanding athlete. "I didn't buy it for that reason," Gerry said. "Morris finds these things and just tells me what he thinks we should do. I'm just trying to stay ahead of inflation."

When Gerry and his barber bought the house, Gerry's attorney suggested a trusteeship that would have kept Gerry's interest out of the public record. Gerry declined. "I wasn't trying to do anything illegal," he said. Gerry's lawyer assured him that it was not illegal. A trusteeship would simply spare him unnecessary criticism. "I wanted everything aboveboard. If I had done that, it would have looked like I was trying to hide something. I didn't want that." As soon as the Francisco family moved in, the gossip began. One public school district was considering filing a written complaint with the OHSAA when Gerry asked for an investigation. At his request the OHSAA looked into the Hiawatha Francisco case and found nothing wrong. "They ought to know I wouldn't do anything dishonest," Gerry said. Nonetheless, he said it was the last time he would help arrange permanent housing for a player's family. "It causes the school and the family too much harassment. No matter what you say, some people won't believe the truth anyway."

The Hiawatha of 1974 was named Kirby Clark. Kirby was running the 100-yard dash under 11 seconds when he was in the eighth grade and was recognized regularly in a local track coaches' newsletter. It was assumed that he would be the next great football player at tiny Lockland High, the smallest city high school in the state. Lockland's varsity football team rarely had more than 30 members, and most of the starters played both offense and defense. But the school had a heroic football tradition; Lockland kids were always tough. Two Lockland grads, in fact, enjoyed professional football careers: Mike Sensibaugh, a defensive back with the Kansas City Chiefs, and Melvin Lunsford, a defensive end for the New England Patriots.

The Clark family did not rent a house from Gerry, but Kirby's dad began driving a new car a year after his son enrolled at Moeller. The rumors had Gerry buying it for him. "Now, where in the heck am I going to get money to buy a guy a car?" Gerry was still asking six years later. "I mean, that's ridiculous!" Lockland High was never in Kirby Clark's future. His parents wanted him to attend a private school and would have sent him to Landmark Christian High, which was operated by their Baptist church, had that school been playing football at the time. Moeller was the next best alternative. Kirby

Clark became one of only three freshmen to play varsity football in Moeller's first 20 seasons. Moeller qualified for the state playoffs all four years Kirby participated, and won three state championships. He also lettered in basketball and baseball. Landmark Baptist Church eventually honored Gerry for his work with Kirby, presenting him with an award for teaching Christian ideals as well as football. Gerry was asked to speak to the Landmark congregation. "It was one of the biggest thrills of my lifetime," he said.

The Moeller district encompassed 11 mostly small public school districts. Virtually every football coach at all of those high schools was convinced that Gerry had stolen at least one good athlete from him at one time or another. But recruiting was not the most important issue in Moeller's own league. "We've always had recruiting in the GCL," league president A. J. Schaub said in 1980. "But nothing, nothing like this." In the Greater Cincinnati League, the issue was much broader. The question was proportion. Objections to many aspects of Gerry's program at Moeller led the other GCL members to draft a league philosophy and code of ethics in 1979. Paragraph by paragraph, the proposals seemed aimed squarely at the biggest and most successful football program in the league, the one that did not lose a league game in eight years from 1973 through 1980.

No member of the GCL fought Moeller more determinedly on the field, or opposed Gerry more vigorously off the field, than Elder, the west side giant. And the Reverend Edward Rudemiller, then Elder's athletic director, was always at the forefront of the Elder assault, challenging Gerry's practices, debating philosophies, and arguing in favor of restrictions that would curb Moeller's dominance in football and restore competitive balance in the league. Father Rudy is a short, cherubic priest who enjoys cigars, a beer on occasion, and sports, especially high school sports. He grew up in Price Hill, where whole families live and multiply for generations without ever changing their zip code, and where Elder has stood since 1923 as a symbol of the area's staunchly Catholic population. Father Rudy attended Elder, played sports for Elder, taught school at Elder, and ran Elder's athletic department for 15 years. He reveled in Elder's successes, but he was in firm disagreement with Gerry and everyone else who suggested that Elder, with almost twice as many boys, could have built a dynasty even greater than Moeller's—in football or any other sport. It was not a question of willingness to sacrifice or work hard for that end, he said, but rather the conviction that such advanced programs do not belong at the high school level.

It was his belief that high school teams should make mistakes and lose with a degree of human regularity. In a brief soliloquy he would quote Vince Lombardi, saying that success demands a singularity of purpose, and then follow up by recalling the reaction of American swimmer Shirley Babashoff, who, after losing four Olympic races to East Germany's Kornelia Ender, said of the East German girl's more demanding regimen: "If that's what it takes to win it all, I don't want it."

About Moeller and Gerry, Father Rudy said: "I never approached athletics for athletics sake. It should be a tool, an instrument in the educational process. The question, philosophically, is one of balance." He asked: "Is it high school football to bring in a team from New York; to play a team from Texas? Is it high school football to play your games in a college stadium? When you travel to places like Cleveland, how many kids get to see the games?" He said: "High school sports is dropping the pass, making the fumble, missing the tackle. They just don't make many mistakes; it's almost impossible to beat them." And he said: "Our league works on the good will of its members. Sometimes one member has to give in for the good of the league. Elder had to agree to do things, or not do things, in the best interests of the league."

But he also said in an interview at his new post in Kettering, Ohio: "Father Krusling and Gerry saved that school. At a time when Moeller was in serious trouble, they made a commitment: Football would be the unifying force in that school. Consider the times. We were coming out of the sixties, and religion was not that popular. People were looking elsewhere for answers. When you're trying to get spiritualistic values across in a materialistic society, the one thing you can get across to kids is athletics. Winning and success are very concrete things. Sacrifice and hard work are very concrete things. You can understand games; they have some stability. I don't think it's so dumb what they did. It saved the school. They built a strong school, with strong support. And football was the rallying point."

Father Rudy also said: "Gerry became a very powerful man. The question when you acquire power is, do you use it to serve or do you use it to exploit? I think Gerry used it to serve. He did a lot for other kids from other schools. He was generous to many people."

But he also said: "Gerry was all for Moeller." And, "It is not healthy for a league when one team wins all the time."

THE END OF AN ERA

GAME SIX: MOELLER vs. ELDER

October 3, 1980

For the mighty Moeller football team, anything less than a victory was a defeat. And for Moeller's frustrated opponents, anything better than defeat was considered a victory. Ties existed only on the scoreboard. Thus, it can be said that Elder came within inches of upsetting Moeller, 21–21, in their 1980 grudge match. It came down to the final 32 seconds, a revealing half minute that exposed the distorted realities of Moeller's preeminence.

Elder scored its third touchdown with a two-minute march, and the teams lined up for the two-point conversion that would decide the game. A pass into a crowd in the right corner of the end zone was batted away by six competing pairs of hands, but interference was called. Elder would get a second chance, this time from a yard and a half. On the Moeller sideline, Gerry turned anxiously and said: "Pray! Everybody pray!" In the stands his daughter Julie was fighting back tears, afraid to watch. "We *can't lose* this game," she said over and over again. Throughout Nippert Stadium 14,000 fans were reacting the same way—as though this conversion attempt could *break* not *make* a tie game. It was an interesting phenomenon.

Standing near Gerry, line coach Steve Klonne was waving furiously, setting the defense with hand signals. In the back of his mind he was thinking, "This is the third time I've been involved like this in one of these Elder-Moeller games." The first time he had come out a loser. Then coaching defense for Elder, he watched Moeller pull out a 24–20 victory. Four years later, after leaving Elder and spending one year at a suburban public school, he found himself on the Moeller end of an almost identical 23–19 Elder near-miss. For this occasion he decided: "I'll call a defense we haven't used all night, just to show them something they haven't seen before and maybe cause a little confusion."

Elder quarterback Harry Westerkamp took the snap and rolled right. The pitchout option was not there, so he knifed toward the

Brother Charles Wanda. *Moeller High School photo.*

Dan Ledford, Moeller's assistant principal and a collaborator with Brother Charles Wanda and Bill Braun on the high school's impressive pep rallies. *Moeller High School photo.*

Bill Braun. *Moeller High School photo.*

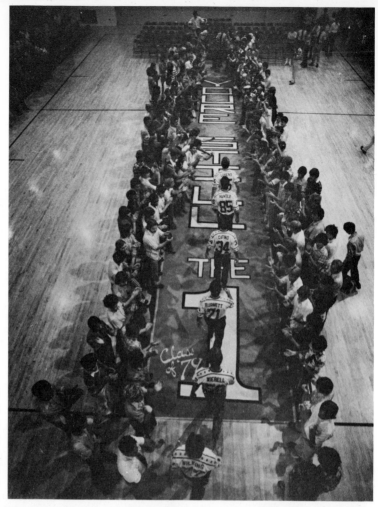

Moeller's elaborate pep rallies attracted huge crowds and always began with the players entering to heroes' welcomes from senior students who lined the entry ramp. *Photo by Ed Reinke.*

Coach Faust takes the microphone during a Moeller pep rally. *Moeller High School photo.*

Gerry presents a banner to Brother Lawrence Eveslage, first principal of Moeller High School. *Moeller High School photo*.

Father Lawrence Krusling, Moeller's principal, knew his students by name and often took time to laugh and joke with them. *Photo by Ed Reinke*.

Gerry's personal ritual on game day always included a pause before the statue of the Blessed Virgin in the school chapel. *Photo by Ed Reinke.*

Senior players always remained for a moment of silent prayer together at the altar after the pre-game Benediction service had ended and their teammates had returned to the locker room. *Moeller High School photo.*

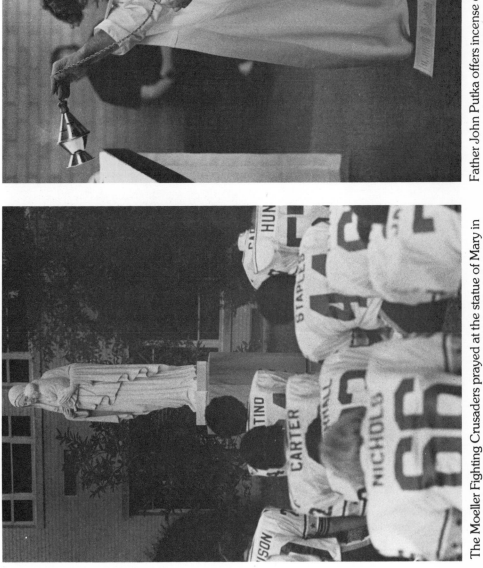

The Moeller Fighting Crusaders prayed at the statue of Mary in the school courtyard each day, before and after every practice or game. *Photo by Ed Reinke.*

Father John Putka offers incense during a pre-game Benediction service for the football team. *Photo by Ed Reinke.*

Gerry yelled at his players a lot, but he laughed with them just as much. *Photo by Ed Reinke.*

Gerry watches intently during pre-game preparations at Nippert Stadium. *Moeller High School photo.*

Coach Gerry Faust in 1964. *Moeller High School photo.*

Gerry's Moeller teams started with hand-me-down equipment and uniforms in the 1960s, but in later years the players and staff were nattily dressed.

Doug Williams, an all-American tackle for Moeller, tries on protective gloves during the first day of practice. Moeller's athletic budget supplied first-class equipment. *Photo by Michael E. Keating.*

Inspirational signs taped to the mirrors in the locker room were a Faust tradition. *Photo by Ed Reinke.*

Moeller students train in a weight room that is the envy of many college athletics programs. Coach Steve Klonne, at left, was twice a "Mr. Cincinnati" runner-up. Student is Tim Dirr. *Photo by Michael E. Keating.*

goal line himself. Moeller defenders swarmed over him; the referee dug to the bottom of the pile, then gave the sign. Westerkamp had been stopped short of the goal line. Gerry gasped, "We almost let this one get away from us." Elder coach Ray Bachus sighed, "I guess it just wasn't meant to be." And as they left the stadium, Moeller fans tried to recover.

"They almost lost!" exclaimed one. "Wouldn't that have been awful," her companion agreed, ignoring the inaccuracy—the worst they could have done was tie.

For a change, it had been a quiet, uneventful week for Gerry, which in retrospect may have saved the season. The lull paid off in Moeller's final eight points—scored with time running out in the first half. Ever daring, Gerry faced a fourth down call at the Elder 30 and sent in tiny Tony Melink, his five-foot-six placekicker, for an apparent 47-yard field goal attempt. But there was confusion in the Moeller huddle. Five yards, delay of game. Gerry was planning a fake kick and Elder appeared unsuspecting.

"Since I had a little time this week," he explained after the game, "I watched some films. I saw how they lined up for kicks and I knew the pass would go." When the field goal team lined up again for a 52-yard kick after the penalty, Elder had adjusted. "They changed defenses when we went back five yards," Gerry said. "They had their block-kick team in before the penalty, then they moved their regular defense in. But I figured, I'll go anyway."

Melink's holder was Ron Lindhorst, the quarterback-turned-tight end. He passed to his alternate at end, Dan Staub, cutting toward the left sideline: 19 yards and a first down. "The thing probably would have gone for a touchdown against their other defense," Gerry fussed.

Six plays later Moeller had its third touchdown, and Melink was back on the field. His last extra point attempt had been slapped back in his face, so Gerry was thinking another fake and pass to make the score divisible by seven once again. "They're going to figure we did it once, we won't do it again," he told himself. Once more: Lindhorst to Staub, wide open for two points to make it 21–7 at the half. No one knew how big that play would prove to be.

Elder was on the ropes at halftime, but the entire Moeller coaching staff was wary. "These Elder kids won't quit," they all warned. "You'd better be ready to take it to them in the third quarter or they'll come back." It was prophetic. Elder scored on its second possession of the second half, but the Panthers' second conversion kick of the game failed just as Moeller's had. The score was 21–13. Suddenly the pressure shifted to the officials, four guys with full-time jobs who spend Friday nights chasing their youth up and down the field for the fun of it. Moeller answered with a long march and an apparent touchdown, but when Mark Brooks lost the ball as he crossed the goal line for the much-needed insurance, the head linesman ruled he lost the ball in the field of play rather than *after* entering the end zone. The ball was recovered by Elder, which made it a touchback. Elder took over with 2:23 left to play, 80 yards away from a possible tie instead of 99.

Game films recorded not only the drama of the final three minutes, but also, in Gerry's opinion, three unforgivable mistakes by the honest men in striped shirts. Brooks had crossed the goal line *before* his fumble, Gerry concluded. It should have been ruled a touchdown. "But the head linesman was two yards out of position to make the call," he said. The pass interference called against Moeller in the end zone was a correct, albeit, close call, "but one of their guards was not set on the last touchdown, and on the second two-point conversion attempt their tailback was in motion. Neither of those were called."

After seeing the films, Gerry did something he never had done before. He fired those officials from a future game. "I sent them all checks for a game we hadn't played yet and told them I'd get a new crew. I signed a contract, so I paid them. They're good people; I just can't have that kind of poor judgment and poor officiating. It could have cost us a game! It could have cost us a spot in the playoffs! It could have cost us thousands of dollars!"

The game had been dedicated to offensive line coach Jim Higgins, who will be remembered forever by less-than-objective Elder fans as the villainous Moeller coach who hit one of their players on an out-of-bounds play in the 1979 game. The incident was indicative of the intensity between Elder and Moeller. A punt return ended along the sideline in front of the Moeller bench. Moeller contended the Elder player continued across the sideline intentionally to crash into anyone he could on the Moeller bench, and that Higgins put up his forearm to fend off the contact when he saw it coming. Elder insisted Higgins hit the boy intentionally, and demanded that the GCL take disciplinary action. League president

Schaub reviewed films and interviewed players, coaches, and officials. He concluded that Higgins did strike the boy and suspended
him for the remainder of the season (two regular-season games and
the playoffs). The incident made newspaper headlines for days.
Behind the scenes there was talk of lawsuits against Schaub, the
league, the archdiocese, and the archdiocesan superintendent of
education, the Reverend Jerome Schaeper. Higgins sat out a 33–0
victory over Roger Bacon that clinched the GCL championship the
next week—Bud Schaub presented the trophy to the Moeller team
after the game. But Father Schaeper, under pressure, then
reinstated Higgins by ruling that decisions made by the GCL president could apply only to GCL games.

Higgins is an intense coach but actually a quiet, gentle man. He
did not mention the previous year's incident all week as Moeller
prepared for Elder. He did not have to. A hand-lettered parchment
scroll, signed by every member of the varsity squad, proclaimed:

> We your 1980 Crusader football team and fellow coaches
> dedicate our game with Elder to you, Coach Higgins, in ap-
> preciation of your dedication, leadership as a coach and fine
> example to all the men of Moeller. Thanks for everything and
> may God bless you always.

A few hecklers congregated outside the Moeller end zone
during pre-game exercises, their taunts just loud enough to be heard
by Higgins and his linemen. "If you're not ready to play after that,"
he said to them, "then nothing will get you ready to play, men."
They were ready. "That's as well as our line can play," Higgins, a
perfectionist, said appreciatively afterward.

In the film *The Longest Day,* Allied and German generals, at
the moment the Normandy invasion is about to begin, simultane-
ously turn to their colleagues in war rooms hundreds of miles apart
and say reassuringly in English and German: "Don't worry! God is
on our side!" Likewise, God was getting it from both sides in the
closing moments of the Moeller-Elder game. And whether He actually interceded or not, defensive end Pat Keneavy and defensive
tackle Tim Dirr made a special postgame request of Father Putka.
Would he open Moeller chapel, they asked their chaplain. The
players and coaches had prayed together before the statue of the

Blessed Virgin in the courtyard outside the school, as they do after every game. But now the seniors wished to give special thanks, solely, silently, privately.

"It's the first time I've ever had a group of players make a request like that after a game," said Gerry, who stayed out of it.

The idea originated with Keneavy. "I was out there on the two-yard line when they scored, and I was out there when they were going for the two-point conversion. You know, when you've gone through summer practice and three years of hard work and it all comes down to the last twenty seconds of a game, you do a lot of thinking and praying. I'll tell you, we said more Hail Marys out there on the field than we did all day. When it was over, we had a lot to be thankful for."

7

'Say a Hail Mary'

Whether it is a born-again Christian telling of his conversion, a self-ordained sidewalk preacher shouting Bible passages, or simply a follower of any faith living it conscientiously and openly, most of society is terribly uncomfortable with public displays of religion. Accordingly, skeptics are suspicious of all the prayer that pervades Gerry's version of the often brutal sport of football. It seems a gigantic contradiction. Actually, it was the most decisive intangible Gerry's Moeller teams possessed. Players, not prayers, win close games, of course. Gerry knows that. But praying does set a tone nothing else can match—in sports or any other activity in life. It is a focal point, a reservoir of strength. It intensifies a person's concentration and fortifies his confidence. Gerry's players believed they would prevail because they had asked for help. But they also believed that, if they did not prevail, they were better prepared to face adversity. "I've never seen a Catholic school that uses the religious aspect so fully to its advantage," said Barry Sollenberger, the man who studies the best high school teams in the country, then ranks them nationally.

Gerry unquestionably is the most prayer-oriented football coach in the world. He led his Moeller teams in prayer—the Hail Mary and The Memorare—countless times before and after every game. They prayed in the locker room and on the team bus, on the practice field and at the stadium, right on the 50-yard line immediately after every game. They prayed in the chapel at school, at the parish church next door to school, and before the statue of Mary in the courtyard behind school. A team Mass was offered once a week, and Benediction and a Scripture reading were regular parts of the pre-game preparation on game day. Gerry scheduled an ecumenical service once or twice each season so the non-Catholic members of the team could invite their ministers to conduct a service for the whole squad. "The purpose," he said, "is to let the other kids show their faith. The point is, there isn't any one faith. Just so long as you believe in a Supreme Being. That's what's important."

Personally, Gerry had his own devotional regimen that included one of Cincinnati's oldest religious customs. The Church of the Immaculata, a beautiful little stone church perched atop a hillside neighborhood called Mt. Adams, overlooks the Ohio River and downtown Cincinnati. Six flights of concrete steps lead to the church door from the street below, and the view from the top is one of the city's best. Each Good Friday, beginning at midnight regardless of the weather, thousands of Cincinnatians climb those steps praying the rosary—one Hail Mary on each step. The practice is repeated occasionally during the rest of the year by individuals with special intentions. For Gerry, that meant twice every week of the season. He prayed the steps each Thursday night before a game, usually accompanied by his captains, and returned in the wee hours following each game, usually alone. It is not an easy devotion to practice, especially so often, and most of Cincinnati had no idea Gerry did it.

On Friday afternoons during the season, Gerry reserved 45 minutes for himself. It was his time to pray and he would not compromise it for anyone or anything. "I have to go to church now," he would say if a request interfered. It was the only time he ever refused anyone. He would walk across the parking lot to All Saints Church, enter through the side door, and shuffle toward the main altar. He would stop for a minute, maybe two, and stare up at the Crucifix, his hand touching the foot of the cross. Then he would move to a statue of the Blessed Mother, again standing in silent prayer for only a few moments. Then it was on to another regular stop in the church. Sometimes a grade school class would be visiting, little voices following a sister's lead in the recitation of a prayer. "Isn't it neat to see those children in church," he would remark happily as he returned to the courtyard for a pause at Mary's feet. Shortly he would move on to the Moeller chapel, where he would pray some more, always in his own words.

"I pray for a lot of things," he explained. "I pray to win; I pray for good weather and a good crowd; I pray that we don't have any serious injuries; I pray for my friends. I just try to talk to Mary and her Son."

The inscription at the base of the statue of Mary in the Moeller courtyard reads, "The true secret of success in any work is to interest the Blessed Virgin in it," and Gerry makes sure he interests her in everything he does. "Say a Hail Mary" was an order given to everyone on the Moeller sideline on every play of importance for 20 years, and Gerry repeats the 41-word prayer dozens of times every day. It flashes through his mind like a recording whenever he has an idle moment.

Gerry's devotion to Mary dates back to the sixth grade when, for the first time in his memory, she answered his prayers. Gerry's team, Our Lady of Mercy, was expected to lose the Dayton CYO championship to St. Joe's Orphanage. In those days the orphanages were filled, a tragic legacy of the Second World War; St. Joe's was loaded with tough kids. Before the big game Gerry and his good friend Russell Sweetman, and all of their teammates, marched into church, knelt around the altar and, with lumps in their young throats, recited:

"Remember, O most gracious Virgin Mary,
That never was it known,
That anyone who fled to thy protection,
Implored thy help or sought thy intercession,
Was left unaided;
Inspired with this confidence,
We fly unto thee, O virgin of virgins, our mother;
To thee we come, before thee we stand, sinful and sorrowful;
O Mother of The Word Incarnate,
Despite not our petitions,
But in thy mercy, hear and answer us,
Amen."

Yes, Our Lady of Mercy beat St. Joe's Orphanage for the city football championship—decisively. Gerry and his buddies played better than they ever had played before, better than they ever thought possible. Their prayer, The Memorare, has been Gerry's favorite ever since.

"You know, people sometimes make fun of athletes praying," he says. "But here I was, a sixth grader really devoutly saying a prayer at the altar, and we're underdogs but we win the game. That left an impact on my life. You might say, 'What if you'd lost?' I still think the impact, the feeling that I felt up at that altar with the rest of those football players, was a feeling of unity with God, and I really, to this day, remember that feeling more than playing any game. I say that prayer every day. It's really a beautiful prayer. If you really sit and listen to the words, it really has a lot of meaning."

Gerry considered a religious vocation before marrying at the age of 29. "I didn't go because I couldn't give up coaching," he says, "so I don't really feel I had a vocation." He may be accomplishing more without one. There is considerable evidence that his example has a lasting impact on those around him. Though he would rather not talk about it, Gerry has contributed to an impressive number of conversions to Catholicism. Just before the start of the 1980 season, one of his senior halfbacks was baptized, and during the season another player, a linebacker who was baptized at birth but had never been a practicing Catholic, received his First Communion. A man Gerry had come to know through Moeller football was taking instruction after years of hesitation, and another friend, who had fallen away from the Church, renewed his faith largely because Gerry's model was so powerfully inspiring. It rings of evangelism, but Gerry makes no attempt to pass himself off as either missionary or saint.

"I really don't like to talk about it," he says. "I don't want to be a hypocrite, and I'm far from a perfect person. I'm tempted many, many times in many, many ways, and the only way I can cope with it is by turning to God. It really plays an important part in my life. I'm not what you'd call a good person, but God's been good to me. I've been a happy person all my life—I've never been a sad person. And when things go wrong, they always work out for the best—maybe not the way I want them to, but they always work out for the best. I've always wondered in life why He's been so good to me, because I really haven't been that good to Him. I just look at the beauty of the whole thing, of what Christ really stands for, why He died on the Cross to forgive our sins and how many chances He really gives us as human beings. I let Him down a lot, but He sticks with me. I really think God looks over me."

Although Gerry and his Moeller teams prayed together for 20

years, no one noticed until they started winning state championships. The first headlines appeared in 1975, when Moeller upset
Lakewood St. Edward, a four-touchdown favorite, 14–12. It was a
grueling game, played on a windswept and raw November night in
Akron's bitter cold Rubber Bowl. Moeller won the game when St.
Edward, relentlessly marching toward the Moeller end zone as the
clock wound down, fumbled inside the Moeller 20 with less than
two minutes left to play. Afterward, Gerry told sportswriters from all
over the state that, in those tense final minutes, he and his players
had prayed to St. Jude, the patron saint of hopeless causes. "We
had lost in the playoffs two years in a row," he said. "That made us
pretty hopeless." With those quotes, an image was born.

Network television and national magazines recorded Gerry's
emphasis on religion extensively during the 1980 season, at one
point dubbing Moeller "The Holy Steamroller." It was convenient,
unique, and very visual. But 15-second film clips of the team singing
at Benediction or Gerry ordering a Hail Mary on the sideline were at
best superficial glimpses of what was taking place. Photographs of
the team praying in the chapel or in front of the statue of Mary
presented an incomplete picture. The context of these scenes was
always missing, and that contributed to a widespread misunderstanding of religion's place in Gerry's coaching style. Twentieth
Century pharisees thought he was just showing off or felt he was
praying for the wrong things. Gerry was criticized a lot for praying.

A few days before Moeller played Massillon in the 1980 state
championship game, one of Massillon's best players was quoted in a
newspaper story, deriding Moeller's religious approach to football.
"I think it's ridiculous for them to pray to win football games," the
boy said. His coach, Mike Currence, who had encountered Moeller's prayer power as Lakewood St. Edward's head coach in 1975,
mocked Moeller's devotion to St. Jude, declaring that the patron of
hopeless causes should be on Massillon's side for this one, since
Massillon was the underdog. Even the Massillon fans had their
irreverent fun, painting large, orange and black signs that read,
"Hail Mary Full of Grace, We Pray Moeller's in Second Place."

Gerry said nothing until game day and then spoke only to his
players. It was one of the best and most important locker room
exhortations of his career. It provided not only incentive but more
importantly perspective. The national media missed it.

"God isn't going to win this football game today," he said with intensity bordering on anger. "Prayer isn't going to win this football game either. God and prayer never win any football game. *You*, the boys in shoulder pads and helmets that we send out on the field, are the only ones who can win this football game. *You* will win it, by playing good, hard, clean, tough football—Moeller football! *You* will win it by thinking and executing and being alert. Prayer will help you play to the best of your ability, but it won't win the game for you. Only *you* can win the game. And you will, because *Moeller* football is the *best* football!"

Priests and brothers within the Marianist community at Moeller held mixed views toward Gerry's melding of football and prayer. All commended the obvious moral and spiritual example set by the coach and his team. But some had problems reconciling those actions with their basic understanding of the Catholic faith. Entirely apart from the issue of whether such beliefs are justifiable as an abstract proposition, they worried that the distinction between a prayer of faith and a superstitious incantation is easily blurred in practice when teen-age boys are asked to recognize the difference intellectually. Was it conscious prayer or were they mumbling magic words?

Father John Putka, who studied in the United States and Switzerland and holds degrees in education, theology, history, and political science, was one of the football team's chaplains during Gerry's last three seasons at Moeller. Father Putka had taught in Marianist high schools in New York, Cleveland, and Dayton, as well as in three colleges and universities. He is a thoughtful man and clever homilist, a perfect choice for his job at Moeller. He is tall, wears a 1950s flat-top, and could have been a guard or tackle himself in another era. He understood athletics and possessed a remarkable faculty for relating religion to sports.

"On a team," he said, "you're really dealing with the fundamental relationships of life. All of these things are necessary in Christianity. It's very easy to tie it in with any sport." Typically, when he spoke to the team on All Saints Day it was more a chat than a sermon.

"Today is the Feast of All Saints," he began, "and you know, men, All Saints Day is for all those people who've made it, who reached their goal of eternal life. And making it—being the best at something—is what Moeller football is all about. It takes hard work, sacrifice, and discipline to make it, on the football field or in life. It isn't easy to make it—in football or in life. The saints we honor today know what it takes, and you do too."

Father Putka pointed out that this Catholic "holy day of obligation" was really for everyone, and he drew a muffled round of good-natured laughter at the expense of one of the Protestant members of the offensive line when he cracked, "All the Baptist saints are watching and praying for Tim Odom right now." There were more chuckles as he told the boys that someday they, too, could "make it." Looking at Gerry he said, "Our reverend coach has a chance. And who knows," he grinned, picking out a rambunctious defensive back in the first row, "someday there might even be a Saint Michael Hartmann, patron of the semi-tough." It was a light sermon on the surface, but everyone in the room got the message. Religion and football again seemed to have a place alongside each other.

Father Putka was not without his own concerns. He even found himself praying feverishly in the tense moments of close games. "I've promised everything but the kitchen sink a couple of times," he confessed sheepishly. If he did that, he wondered, could the boys possibly be praying for anything more?

"Gerry's sincerity is so complete he can do what he does," Father Putka said. "But I don't think the kids will really understand the role of prayer in their lives until they experience more of life. Prayer in this context is open to misunderstanding. If the other team is better, what you're really asking God to do is work a miracle. If the boys think God's going to work all those minor miracles, they're wrong. But at least they're learning to turn to God, to talk to Him. They're learning to pray for help. With this experience, they should be more inclined to pray the rest of their lives."

Once, maybe, God did work a miracle for Gerry. At least Gerry thinks so. On a dog-day afternoon in August 1979, during a routine workout at summer practice, a handsome, dark-haired freshman defensive tackle named Mike Susshine collapsed. Comatose, he was rushed to the nearest hospital, and one of the Moeller physicians, Doc Kollman, was summoned. There was no news until the doctor emerged from the intensive care unit. He was crying.

"Doc, how is he doing?"

"Gerry, he isn't going to make it. He's got a hundred-and-eight temperature, and we can't get it down. We don't know what's wrong."

Gerry asked for odds, and Doc Kollman answered:

"One percent chance of survival."

Gerry sagged under the weight of those words, then looked at his friend. Softly, he said:

"Doc, he's going to make it, because we're going to pray."

Gerry found the boy's parents, called a couple of priests, and went to the hospital chapel. They stayed for hours, praying to the patron of the impossible, St. Jude. Hours later the patient's temperature dropped and doctors improved the odds on his survival to 50–50. But no one would guess at the extent of his recovery. Brain damage was the unspoken fear.

More long days and nights passed, the parents never leaving their son. And then, one day, Mike Susshine woke up. Months later he was participating in 10-mile hikes, making honor roll grades, and was cleared to try football again if he wished, though it was agreed he would not. A metabolism problem had almost cost his life; prayer, it would seem, helped save it.

"There's no doubt in my mind," Gerry said, "that was a miracle."

THE END OF AN ERA

GAME SEVEN: MOELLER vs. ST. XAVIER

October 10, 1980

Gerry Faust and Steve Rasso, the St. Xavier coach, have been friends for a long time. When Steve was being pressured out of his job at LaSalle, Gerry stood up for him. When Steve got out of coaching and then wanted to get back in, Gerry went to bat for him. When Moeller made it to the state playoffs the first time, Steve scouted possible state championship game opponents for Gerry, and when the chorus of coaches criticizing Gerry and Moeller grew louder, Steve was still heard saying, "But wait." In coaching, though, even the most durable friendships are hard-pressed to survive the unforgivable sin of the profession—running up the score. Whether real or imagined, that had become an issue between Gerry Faust and Steve Rasso in recent years. And 1980 was not destined to be the year that it went away.

It started in 1978, Rasso's first year as head coach at St. X. "They had an outstanding team and we were average," is Steve's version. "The score at the half was like 30–0, definitely under control. He came out with his 'ones' in the third quarter, which didn't bother me. But when he scored again, he kept them in. He wanted more points." The final score was 48–7. "I had a hard time with that, especially being a friend. I mean, I can see pouring it on some team from the other end of the state, but you don't do that to your friends!"

Steve and Gerry talked it over. "I told him I didn't try to run up the score on him, but if he thought I did, then I apologize," Gerry said. The next season was not quite as bad. Moeller won, 34–0. Again, Gerry "didn't think he ran the score up," Steve said, and he gave him the benefit of the doubt. But the memory lingered as 1980 arrived with Moeller unbeaten in six games, and St. Xavier on a five-game winning streak after losing its season opener.

Before the game, there was an incident; early in the game, another.

Gerry: "I went to see him at his thirty. He grabbed me by the arm, pulled me away, and said, 'We'll talk at the fifty, Gerry!' "

Steve: "I don't want him coming into our group. It's a matter of the distraction, our guys trying to get ready and seeing him among them."

The game began and there was a mixup getting a ball into play from the sidelines.

Gerry: "He threw our ball boy off his sideline! Can you imagine that!"

Steve: "He doesn't have to have a ball boy on our side of the field. We don't send a ball boy to the other side of the field for our home games."

Symbolically, there were storm clouds building in the evening sky; the horizon was flickering to the southwest. "The rain's coming," Gerry mumbled anxiously. No rain ever fell, but lightning struck four times on the field in the first quarter.

3:47 to play—Defensive back Alex Ditullio of St. Xavier intercepts a pass and returns it 47 yards for a touchdown. The stunned Moeller sideline is silent.

3:01—On the second play after the St. X touchdown, Moeller's Mark Brooks starts into the right side of the line, veers left toward the outside, cuts back behind a block and is into the open field, chased by Alex Ditullio. Seventy-seven yards, touchdown, tie score.

3:01—Moeller kicks off. The St. X receiver fumbles and Moeller recovers on the St. Xavier 21.

2:36—First play from scrimmage after the fumble. Moeller's Tim King on a double reverse, 21 yards, touchdown.

The half ended, 14–7. Brooks broke loose for 73 yards early in the third quarter and scored again with 7:11 left in the game. St. Xavier was unable to move against the Moeller defense all night. At 28–7, "the game definitely was under control," recalls Steve Rasso. Time to play the second-stringers, he felt. Gerry alternated substitute running backs, but the rest of the first team stayed in the game. Moeller drove for one more touchdown in the final minutes, punter Jim Rohlfs scoring from fullback on a short run with 52 seconds left in the game. "That blew my mind!" Rasso said. "I have a hard time with that, but that's him. He hadn't beaten many teams bad. He needed it."

When a football game ends, the opposing coaches usually meet somewhere near midfield to shake hands, even if they do not particularly like each other or if the loser does not feel especially good about losing. Steve Rasso went straight to the St. Xavier locker room, stopping only long enough to speak momentarily to Moeller assistant Ted Bacigalupo. "He ran the score up again!" Steve shouted. "You tell him when I vote in the state poll this week I won't even rank Moeller in the top ten!" In fact, after he cooled down, Rasso voted for Moeller anyway.

As Steve steamed away, Mark Brooks was being interviewed across the field by a sportswriter, Coach Faust at their side. Brooks had broken one of Moeller's oldest school records by rushing for 254 yards. It beat former Ohio State fullback Randy Keith's record set in 1969 by 41 yards. Brooks had been a preseason high school All-American but had been largely unimpressive the first half of the season. The sportswriter wanted to know why. Gerry helped Mark with the answer.

"He was overweight and out of shape when he reported to summer practice! Tell him Mark!"

"I was out of shape and a little overweight."

"He didn't work as hard in the off-season as some of the other players did. So he had to run; we ran him extra every day, but not to punish him. Tell him Mark!"

"I had to run a lot to get in shape because I didn't work as hard as I should have."

Gerry was not really trying to speak for his star. He does not restrict any of his players. His answers were his way of expressing the pride he felt in seeing this athlete excel. Chiding him about what he had to overcome was a way of recognizing the effort Brooks had put forth, a reminder of what he had done rather than a reminder of what he had failed to do. How did Brooks really feel about all of those extra laps? "They did the same thing to Eric Ellington last year," he said. "I figured if he could take it, I could take it."

Winning a football game has seldom been less enjoyable for Gerry than it was that night. He returned to Moeller rambling to himself about his encounters with Steve Rasso. "Why'd he have to do what he did before the game? I'm not going to steal any secrets . . . *Nobody* trusts us! . . . And why'd he have to throw our ball boy off their sideline? Beckstedt's no spy! . . . And after the game he just takes off for the locker room—doesn't make any effort to see me!"

"Don't worry about it," shrugged Steve Klonne. "He's just tired of getting beat by us."

"It's lonely at the top, Gerry," chided another friendly voice.

Gerry smiled. "Yeh, I guess it is. But it's still the only place to be, right men?"

There was a chorus of agreement. "Especially after you've been at the bottom," Pat Orloff offered dryly, his days of struggle in an unsuccessful public school program still vivid in his memory.

Next morning, when the coaching staff assembled at Moeller to review films of the St. X game and begin preparing for the next one, Gerry was still fretting over his differences with Steve Rasso. "I didn't run up the score," he insisted, whether or not anyone was listening. "I have an obligation to this team to build its momentum . . . Jim Higgins wanted to keep the first line in there because the 'twos' didn't know the blocking schemes." Almost as an afterthought, he added: "If Steve was interested in playing everyone, why did he keep his first team in on defense?" And, "I've had people score a lot of points on me. That's part of the game. You have to forget about it."

While Gerry was meeting with the team, a St. Xavier assistant coach called the Moeller athletic department. The St. X camera had malfunctioned and their game film was lost. Could St. Xavier borrow Moeller's film? Gerry puzzled over that one. "I don't have anything against the kids," he reasoned. "I don't want to penalize them. They're welcome to the film. But there's a principle involved here." The St. X coach would be calling back; the Moeller coach who had taken the message wanted to know what to tell him.

"Tell him if Steve will call me in person, he can have the film. I'd like to talk to him."

8

The Motivational Speaker

Speaking to the well-dressed men and women of the business world, Gerry came on a little like Columbo, the disarming television detective who disguised his brilliance in a rumpled raincoat. It was not unusual for Gerry to face an audience of pin-striped suits and designer dresses wearing tan work pants and a pullover open-neck knit shirt with the words "Moeller Coaching Staff" over the heart. The skeptics in his captive audiences would wonder at the sight. What did our corporate geniuses bring us this time? But when he had finished, they would stand in line to shake his hand, applaud him with standing ovations, and, in some cases, even break into tears. The chief executive officer of Medenco, a hospital insurance company in Houston, offered him an executive position with the company after hearing him speak. There were other job offers, too.

Gerry's talks were crammed with common sense advice, old-fashioned precepts, and inspirational stories about the Men of Moeller. His message was not unique: think positive, plan ahead, organize better, work together, work hard but have some fun, respect your fellow man, and worship your Creator. The difference was sincerity, enthusiasm, and his own success using the formula he was endorsing. He expressed himself in convoluted sentences sprinkled with misused words; no phony eloquence, no fancy polish. He was conversational and entertaining; secure, confident, and completely at ease. He could have been standing in a locker room rather than a plush hotel's banquet hall or some exclusive resort's

111

auditorium. He could have been speaking to fellow coaches at a clinic rather than sales executives, personnel directors, office managers, or management consultants. Their business was insurance or manufacturing or finance or marketing; his business was football. He was paid $1,500 to translate his approach to their use. Most of them, as children, had been told the same things by their parents—at no charge.

Gerry spoke to his first business audience in 1977. A friend at Procter & Gamble called him in a panic when a scheduled speaker cancelled at the last minute. Gerry addressed a sales meeting, and his pep talk was so good the guy at P&G told a friend at IBM. Referrals increased. Pretty soon Frederick Klein of the *Wall Street Journal* called. He wanted to do a story for the nation's most prestigious business newspaper about the nation's newest motivational speaker. After "A Pep Talk To Remember" was published, Gerry's phone rang continuously. Companies large and small, church groups, and civic groups wanted him to speak. He increased his fee to discourage requests because it was taking too much of his time, but companies simply met his higher price. He spoke for IBM 10 times in one year.

He tried to be away from home and Moeller for no more than 36 hours at a time, flying as far as the West Coast and back without a night's stay if he could make plane connections. His itinerary criss-crossed the continent: Acapulco . . . Boston . . . Chicago . . . San Juan . . . Seattle . . . Houston . . . Philadelphia . . . Portland . . . Dallas . . . Hilton Head . . . Miami . . . Denver. . . . He traveled a hundred thousand miles in a year.

A 10-minute color movie introduced everyone to Gerry's world, the world of Moeller football. It was professionally done and very effective. Hundreds of color slides of the Moeller program flashed across the screen during the fast-paced encounter that followed. Gerry was always in motion, pacing back and forth across the front of the room and advancing slides as he talked. He never changed his basic material; he merely adapted it to suit the audience. He usually spoke for more than an hour—always without notes—and never missed a chance to relate a point to his audience by injecting the host company's name or product into an example. A speech given at a management development seminar for employees of Blue Cross of Southwest Ohio, a medical insurance company, was representative of his motivational talks:

"If you're wondering why a football coach has come to talk to you today, since you're in the business world, I think that after I'm finished you'll find out that there isn't much difference between the business world and me coaching football, because one thing is in common—we're *both* dealing with *people,* and *that's* the *key* to *life.* It's how you work with people, how you motivate people, how you deal with people that is the success that you as a person, you as a company, can derive from. It's all there, and I'll tell you, I think that when we're finished, we'll find out that your job and my job are very, very similar.

"I'm very proud of Moeller High School; I'm very proud to be a part of Moeller High School; I'm very proud to represent Moeller High School. That's why every time I go somewhere I try to wear something with Moeller on it. I'm very proud of it, not because of its football prowess, but because it is a great school academically, discipline- and moral training-wise. I've been with the school since its existence twenty years ago, and just to be a part of a great institution like that really means something to me. And it should mean the same to you with Blue Cross. You should have the same feeling. If you *don't,* then you should get out and get another job, because you're not doing Blue Cross a favor, you're not doing yourself a favor and you're not doing your family a favor, because you're going to come home frustrated. If you don't like what you're doing, if you're not proud of the company that you represent, then you look for something else, because you're not going to fulfill what you're doing, you're not going to fulfill the company what they're asking you to do. *That's* the way you've *got* to *feel.* It's got to be part of you.

"And another thing that's important: you've got to love to work with people. You are in a people-oriented type business, just like I am. I love kids. I love being around kids. Some of the kids some-times don't think I like them, but I'm just trying to do the best for them, and that's the same with the people you're working with. I'm sure there's times that the people you supervise don't like the decisions you make, don't like what you tell them to do. But if you're really sincerely interested in doing a good job, then, by golly, they'll see through that and they'll have that respect that's necessary.

"You know, another thing that I think is very, very important is that you've got to feel you're doing something worthwhile. And working with young people, I really feel that you can really help generate their way of life. And you've got the same thing. You're helping people unbelievably, and you don't even know it. You're helping people by making sure that they have a good medical policy, and then, in that time when people have to use the policy, they're under stress because either something is wrong with them or their loved one, and if they've got the proper medical coverage that will take care of the financial burden of it. *Then* you're helping relieve those people of some of the problems that they have.

"Now, how do you do it *better?* Well, you do it better by being organized better, and by doing things better to keep the cost down, to be more efficient, so that when the person takes their policy and uses it, they get coverage, they get the payment right back. And *that* takes . . . *teamwork!* That's what it's all about. All you in here are in a supervisory capacity, and that is a pat on the back, because you wouldn't be in that unless you had the ability to lead. So therefore, you're a winner, as far as I'm concerned. That's what I call a winner, a person that has the ability to be a leader or run something or supervise. That's a leader. *But* . . . are you a *champion?* That's the question I'm asking you.

"You know, it takes a lot more to be a champion than just a winner. And you know what it is? It's a *little* thing, getting down and doing the little things in life. The little things in your job make the difference between being a winner and being a champion. This is what we try to do at Moeller with our football players and our athletes. We try to do the little things and make them champions. And I think that's the *difference!* Because there are a lot of schools that are winners, and a lot of kids that are winners in life, and a lot of athletes are winners, but the thing is, *are they champions?* It's by them learning to do the little things and wanting to do the little things better that they become champions.

"I bet most of you have paperwork, because I think your job is almost all paperwork orientated. My job is, too, believe it or not, and I hate it, hate all the paperwork. And I bet you do, too. But you know, I get down and I push myself to do it and do it right. Because I don't want to leave anything for chance. I want to have everything down just exactly right. I don't want to cheat those kids in any way whatsoever. And you don't want to cheat your company or fellow worker, or the people that subscribe to Blue Cross. You don't want to do that either, and so therefore, you've got to give that little extra to be the champion.

"There's a couple of models that we try to use at Moeller High School that I think are very, very important. And I think also they're very important as far as your job. One of them, we have a rule—I have a rule—that I never treat anybody any different than I'd want to be treated myself. And I think that's really important. So, when you're handling someone, if you think before you talk to them, you give them constructive criticism or praise, then find out, think to yourself how you would want to be treated, before you do it. Take a little time. A lot of times when you're angry, that really helps you out. Take a little time to say, 'How would I want to be treated in this situation?' And ninety-nine percent of the time, if you do it how you want to be treated, you'll do it the right way.

"The other thing is that if you're going to correct somebody and it's under an emergency situation, then you have to do it right on the spot, like in a game. But, if you get on a person and get on a person and get on a person, you're going to destroy him. You've got to sit down and go to a spot and talk to them after they've cooled off—after you've cooled off. Sit down and go through it on a one-to-one basis and get it solved that way. I'll tell you, I can take an athlete, a great athlete—and you can do the same with someone working for you—I can take a great athlete and destroy him in five minutes. Destroy him. Destroy his confidence which takes years and weeks to build. Confidence is the greatest thing a person can have, and you can do the same thing with the people you work with. You can destroy their confidence in five minutes, just by harping on them a certain way and getting on them. And you don't solve anything by that. You *must* use a *positive* approach in everything you do.

"I became positive back in 1968 and I really learned a lesson in that year. In 1968 we were getting ready for the season with eight senior starters. It was the worst season we ever had. Yet, probably the most gratifying. We were six-two-and-two that year. Yet I thought we did the best job of coaching that year and the kids gave us the most they had. But the thing was, in the opening of practice I turned to one of my fellow coaches, about the third or fourth day, and said, 'This is going to be the worst football team Moeller has ever had.' Just by watching them practice. And, you know, one of the kids heard me say that, and I could never rectify that. I could never rectify that at all. I learned a lesson right then. First of all, if you think that way on the side, you never say it. You think positive all the time and you act positive all the time.

"This year we were at practice and our passing game wasn't that great. Our coaches were coming in and saying, 'The boys are not throwing the ball well, and the kids aren't catching it.' I got with the coaches and said, 'Listen, we've got to solve it, but we're not going to solve it by being negative.' I've never been negative since

1968. Every team that's been up there since then, I tell them that they're going to be the greatest team that ever walked on the earth. And, you know something, they start to believe that, and they start to do things right, and they act that way. Confidence is the greatest thing in the world. You can be an average athlete and if you get confidence in yourself, you're going to be a better athlete. The same with your job. You can be average, but with confidence you're better. So, anyhow, this year I told the coaches this: I said, 'We're going out there and we're going to take the blame for the passing game. We're going to change our concept in the practice schedule. We're going out there and everything we teach those kids is going to be on a positive note. I don't want anybody getting chewed out, and if they drop the ball, tell them if they would have looked and watched the ball a little longer, they would have caught it. The quarterback throwing the ball—if you would have just released it a little quicker, the ball would have gone at that angle better.' And you know, they started to catch on. This was in the sixth and seventh games of the season, but we knew we had to have a passing game for the playoffs. And so, by golly, it got better and better. We got into the playoffs and we threw the ball thirty-two times, completed nineteen passes for six touchdown passes. We had a really unbelievable passing attack in the playoffs because the kids really believed it. By positive action, positive thinking, we got the kids going in the right direction. They started to believe in themselves.

"Have you ever had a day when you get up in the morning and something goes wrong and you say, 'Jimminy, it's going to be one of those days.' I bet you do that a lot; I've done it. But you know what I say now? 'Well, it started out bad but it's still going to be a great day.' And you'd be amazed how it turns around. Because it's just how you think—a lot of it's all in your mind. You may not think so, but I'll tell you. It really does occur.

"Last year we got beat by Princeton, the first time we got beat in seven years, thirteen to twelve on a thirty-seven-yard field goal with seven seconds to go in the game. I'll never forget it. Those kids had won fifty-three straight games, so you know what we told them? I was honest with the kids, because I believe in honesty. I sat down with the seniors and I said, 'You'll always have the stigma of being the team that broke the winning streak, that you were on the team that lost after fifty-three games. But you can also have the thing of being the team that started a longer winning streak. We've got eight games left in this season; you win eight and we'll carry it on and get more than fifty-three games.' And by golly, they won eight straight. So each year we tell the seniors they owe it to that class to get that winning streak longer.

"Our seniors are our leaders. And that's the same with you. You're the supervisors; you put yourself in the seniors' position. They've got to be leaders. They're the ones that set the tone, and those other kids look up to them. That's the same with you. You set the tone in your office. You set the tone. And how you act is how the people underneath you act also, and how they work. I talk to the whole team and tell them about goals, and I talk to them individual-ly, because I think it's also important to have individual goals. I take each kid and talk to him for about two or three minutes and tell him what I think he can do that year and what I think he should try to do that year, and how he's going to be important to the team. And so this kid then has individual goals. But we never want those individ-ual goals to supersede the team goal, just like here.

"We have offense, defense, kickoff team—things like that. They're all separate units. You can have a problem if the game's tight and you come back and blame it on the other. 'Well, the kicking team didn't play well. The offense didn't play well.' We don't let them do that. It's a team, and that's just like when some-thing goes wrong at Blue Cross. You can't blame the accounting department, the computer department, or the public relations de-partment. It's a team. You've all got to work together. You can't blame one department or the other; you've got to get together and solve the whole thing. You've got to work as a team; every depart-ment has to work together. I'll tell you, you'd be surprised if you work together and forget these petty jealousies and forget these things of 'Well, it was their fault or his fault' and take the blame yourself, and start improving. You'd be surprised how much better you'll all become, the whole Blue Cross team. And that's the important thing, see, the end result of what the whole team does, not what one department does. Just like the offense or defense. It's a whole team, and that's what we try to stress."

Gerry's slide show moves to Bill Clark's Weight Room, ballet classes, quickness drills, and the Hall of Champions where every scholarship winner and award winner is listed by name and senior year.

"You've got to do things like this, see. You've got to think, and you've got to work and try to improve. You can never be satisfied with what you've done. You've always got room for improvement.

And that's what you've got to do as a supervisor. Never be satisfied—be happy you've done a good job, but then go on to bigger and better things.

"Last year Rick Boone, who played back in 1969, came in to me and said his name was not up on our Hall of Champions board, and he had won an award. I went in and got the machine and put it up right then. Because that meant something to him. You, as department heads and supervisors, should have some kind of an award that you give out each year. It's got to be worthwhile, and it's got to be sincere. And if it has those two things and you give it to someone, and they justly deserve it, you can't believe what that means to a person. All of us need a pat on the back once in a while. We all do. It's important that we get a pat on the back.

"In our locker room we have all kinds of mirrors, and on every mirror we've got a little saying: 'My God, let me live this day as though I knew it were my last.' This was not made by me; this was made by a kid that played quarterback for us. He made these up at his own expense when he was in college, to put on cars. Well, three months after he got those made up, he got killed in an airplane crash. We lost three football players in the early seventies in a Marshall University plane crash. There's no doubt in my mind that Bob's in Heaven, no doubt about it at all, because this is the way he felt before God took him. I feel that God figured he did what he had to do on Earth and He wanted him to be with Him. But our kids go back and comb their hair every night, and when they're combing their hair, I want them to realize why they're really here on earth. I want them to think that this may be their last day. How would *you* want to live your *last* day here on earth? I think it's important to sit and analyze that. You've got to not only look at the present, but you've got to look at the future.

"In your job you've got to be planning ahead. When you go in and you talk to the people you're working for, don't go in off the cuff; go in prepared. You're hurting yourself and you're hurting the people you're working for if you're not prepared. We even teach our kids how to come out before a game. Because we want that opponent down at the other end, when they're watching us and they see us break a ninety-degree cut like that and we're doing everything exactly right, we want them thinking, 'Hey, that's Moeller! Look at those guys!' That's six points in our favor right there; we're six points up before the game starts. Psychology is a great thing.

"When we tell our kids to be first class, we're going to treat them first class. And, by golly, Blue Cross is asking you to be first class. If you aren't getting first-class supplies, first-class this and that, whatever you need, then you should go to someone higher than you and say, 'Hey'—and be nice about it—'you're asking me to do a first-class job; all I'm asking you to do is give me first-class equipment.' And you know what? In the right mind, they should do that. If they can. It's important. We tell our kids we want them to give a hundred and twenty percent, so we're going to give them a hundred and twenty percent. We have sixteen doctors come and give physicals. There's no other high school around that has this. And you know, it saves Blue Cross a lot of money; I'll tell you, a lot of money. It keeps those policies down.

"Now, in our school—it's predominantly Catholic—we have about a hundred and fifty kids who go there who aren't Catholic, kids of every faith. Once a year we have an ecumenical service. I'd say twenty of the two hundred kids in the football program aren't Catholic, so once a year I bring in a preacher or a reverend from another church. Two years ago we had a preacher from Landmark Baptist come over, and I'm telling you he was a fire-and-brimstone guy. . . . He got up there and he did that service, and I'm telling you, if I wasn't Catholic I'd have been a Baptist the next day. He had me so fired up, it was unbelievable! The neat thing about it is, we sit down and talk about all these things together, and it's good to communicate that way. It doesn't matter what faith you belong to, as long as you believe, as long as you believe in a Supreme Being. That's all that counts. The way you do it—that's your business. Because if you want to really get down and analyze the whole thing, we all believe in the same Person, we just do it a little differently.

"I'm going to tell you something right now. If the country and the world was run like our locker room, like our football team, there wouldn't be any problems, because our kids could care less what color you are, what faith you are, where you come from—all they want to do is be together and be a team and work together. Five years ago we had a kid who transferred, who was going to the school we were playing that night. He got up and spoke to the team that night; now he could have stayed at that school if he'd wanted to, because he started at that school, but he opted to come to Moeller High School. So he got up and he said, 'You know, I'm the second-string quarterback as a senior here at Moeller. I could be the starting quarterback for the other team tonight.' And this was a tough game—we had to win this game to get in the playoffs. So he got in there and he said, 'I could be the starting quarterback, but I wouldn't trade playing second-string quarterback for Moeller for anything in the world, for two reasons. One, I'm playing for the best, and I'm so proud that I'm part of Moeller football.' And me, I'm back there crying. He says. 'The second reason is, this is a real family. I want to thank you guys for making me part of that family in two short years.' Well, boy, I'm really crying then. I go down to the locker room, and I'm the last guy in the locker room—this is a honest-to-God true story. I walk in the locker room and who's at the door? Our first-string quarterback, Jay Rains. Jay comes up to me and says, 'Coach, start Marty tonight.' And I said, 'Jay, you're our best so we're going with you because we've got a rough game tonight, and we've got to win this game.' And he said, 'Coach, Marty will be your best tonight.' I said, 'Okay, Jay, go back and tell Marty.' So Jay went back and told Marty. He said, 'I asked Coach Faust to start you Marty, because you made me a better quarterback. You pushed me for two years.' Marty gave Jay a hug, and Jay gave Marty a hug. It's the greatest thing I've ever seen. He'd given up his starting position in maybe the last game of his career for a teammate. Well, anyhow, Marty Klotz went out and the first play of the game he threw a seventy-eight-yard touchdown pass, and we won 40–0. If the world was run like that, it would be a beautiful place to live, a beautiful place. And then we'd have fun.

"I think it's important to have fun. You can't ask the people in your department to work, work, work. They've got to have fun once in a while. It's not really work when you love something. We love it. And I hope you do the same in your job, because if you do, it's fun. Now, you've got to put yourself on their level once in a while. That's important, too. You're going to sit down and laugh at me. Do you know what I do? I go into the locker room every night and I sit down with the kids. I go with a different group of kids each day, sit on the bench while they're undressing, and talk, shoot the bull with them after practice. You'd be amazed at what I find out. You'd be amazed, just by sitting there and laughing. I find out why John isn't practicing so well, because his girl friend broke up with him two nights ago. And I never would have known that. So, I start to keep my eye on John. I told him, 'I hear you got shot down, John. Well, that's the first time, but there will be twenty more times before it's over with.' And when you start kidding them that way, they get out of it. Not only that, you sit there talking to the kids on a friendly basis after you've been out there really pushing them, and you'd be amazed at how they really like this. And so, when you get to know your fellow employees better, that really helps out, too. Sit there and talk to them. Find out—just shoot the breeze. They may not produce so well because they may have a problem at home that is unbelievable. Or they may have someone sick. Maybe you can help out in some sincere way. I think that's important.

"We dedicate the game to a different person each week. People that have helped us out, people who have supported the program, people less fortunate than us. One young man has been blind since birth. He's got four brothers that were managers at Moeller High School. He went to the School for the Blind up in Columbus. He's one of our closest backers; he goes everywhere with us. He gets down in the locker room after the game, plays the harmonica and everybody starts dancing and singing—he's just great. The kids love him. We dedicated a game to him in braille, and it really meant something to him. But you know who really benefits from it? The kids. The kids that are there benefit from seeing this, that they're doing something good for somebody else.

"You know, when those people are gone, I sit the kids down and I tell them. 'There go I, but for the grace of God.' Did you ever sit down and think about that? 'There goes you, but for the grace of God.' How many of you get up every day and complain? How many of you every day have something to gripe about? I do it. I'm sure you do it. But, I'm doing less of it, the older I get, because you know what? You sit down and see what you've got—you live in a great country; you work for a great company, Blue Cross; you've got a great job; you've got your health. What more can you ask for? You think you've got problems? You come with me and I'll show you someone who's got problems twice as bad as yours. Instead of complaining, get down on your knees every night and thank God for what you've got. Do less complaining and be more positive, and you're going to be a better person."

The speaking engagements proved to be more than a lucrative sideline. Influential Notre Dame alumni were executives in many of the companies that hired Gerry to speak. They were impressed. Gerry was personable, dynamic, exciting—all of the qualities the alumni wanted in their next head football coach. In a way these speeches were auditions, and Gerry was becoming a star.

THE END OF AN ERA

GAME EIGHT: MOELLER vs. ROGER BACON

October 17, 1980

The telephone started ringing on Wednesday: first a paper in New Jersey; then Bill Gleason, sports editor of the Chicago *Sun-Times;* then someone from the *Harvard Crimson,* the campus daily; and finally, "the gentleman from *The Times,"* in this case Gordon S. White, Jr. Gerry was trying to get his football team ready to play Roger Bacon for the Greater Cincinnati League championship, and these people kept calling and asking about the Notre Dame job.

"You know why I'm calling, don't you," Gleason said with a knowing laugh halfway through his interview. He had just quizzed Gerry on basic biographical information: age, 45; wife, Marlene; children, Julie, Gerry, and Steve; father, Fuzzy Faust, a teacher for 50 years and an immensely successful coach himself.

"No, why are you calling?" Gerry replied sincerely.

"Because you're going to be the next head coach at Notre Dame!" Gleason blurted. "Congratulations!"

Gerry said, "I wish you'd tell me your source so they could tell me," and "Mr. Gleason, you're really sticking your neck out if you write that."

Bill Gleason thanked Gerry for the interview and reported in Friday's editions: "For the first time in 26 years Notre Dame will turn over direction of its football program to a high school coach. Barring unlikely outside interference by prominent alumni, the university soon will announce the appointment of Cincinnati's Gerry Faust as successor to Dan Devine . . ."

Harvard coach Joe Restic, meanwhile, had been declared winner of the Irish Sweepstakes by the Quincy (Massachusetts) *Patriot-Ledger* in Thursday's editions, and many eastern papers picked up on the story. "A guy from Harvard's school paper called me at eleven-thirty Thursday night," Gerry said. "He asked me if Joe Restic had accepted the job!" Accustomed to more outrageous late-night calls than this one, Gerry laughed it off. "Why don't you call Joe and ask him?" he suggested. "I don't even know the man."

By Friday afternoon Gordon White was in South Bend to cover the next day's game between the unbeaten Irish and Army. He caught Gerry in the coaches' office on his fourth call. "There's no doubt about it," he assured. "You've got the job."

Gerry had written a three-sentence statement after Gleason's call, but he did not bother to read it to White. "It's news to me," he said weakly. "If I got the opportunity I'd be more excited than the man who wins the presidency, but to be honest with you, I have not been formally offered the job. No one has spoken to me yet."

In the Saturday *New York Times,* Gordon White wrote: "The University of Notre Dame has decided to hire Gerry Faust, a successful high school coach in Cincinnati, to succeed Dan Devine as football coach at the end of the season, according to a source in the department of athletics . . ."

Gerry had not mentioned the words Notre Dame in the presence of the Moeller varsity even once during the two months since summer practice began. "I'm proud of myself," he confided one day. "I haven't said a thing to Williams or Brooks or Mike Larkin about going to Notre Dame if I get the job. A lot of coaches would be talking to their best kids about coming along if they thought they might be going into college. But I don't think that's right. I want to wait until after the season and see if I get the job, first." The time had come, however, for Gerry to address the situation with his players, though he still would manage to avoid all references by name. They assembled at the statue of the Blessed Virgin.

"I haven't said anything all year, and I wasn't going to," he began, "but there's a story out now. It was in a Chicago paper today, and it will be in all the papers tomorrow. But there's no truth to it. I haven't talked to them; I haven't negotiated with them. I'm not interested in that right now. I'm only interested in winning a league championship tonight, going thirteen-and-zero and winning another state championship. I'm being honest with you. I don't know what will happen—I might get it and I might not. But I do know nothing has happened yet. I can't let any personal ambitions I have come first. You guys have worked too hard. I'm here to go all the way with you, and that's all I care about."

When there's ink on newsprint, the television cameras are never far behind. Not in Cincinnati. By late afternoon, two-man, interviewer-photographer teams literally stood in line in the crowded office shared by Moeller's 18 coaches. Patiently, Gerry recounted the previous two days, phone call by phone call. Enduringly, he repeated his honest denial. "Just newspaper talk," he said more than once with an uncomfortable grin. One struggling reporter, in desperation, asked finally: "Why do you *think* Bill Gleason would write a story like this?" Throughout the TV interviews, Gene Caddes, United Press International, sat off in a corner, taking notes. He left without asking a question of his own. It simply was not necessary.

The strain was showing, more than it had all season. As the lights went out on the last interview, Gerry sequestered himself in the film room: peace and quiet for 10 minutes, a chance to reflect. "You know," he thought aloud, "I don't even know if I'll take the job if they offer it to me. I probably will, but we still have a lot to talk about." There was the question of his salary, and the size of his staff, and salaries for his assistants. He had not talked terms. "I really wish everyone would forget about it for now," he said wearily. "I wish it would go away until the season is over."

Heavy rain and thunderstorms were forecast by evening, continuing through the night. The weather only compounded the anxiety that enveloped Gerry. "The timing is terrible," he said. "We have a game to play—a tough game for the league championship—and it's going to rain. Anything can happen when it rains; and how can you expect these kids to concentrate with something like this going on?" He asked each player to bring two towels from home. "Tell your mom you want the oldest ones she's got, and tell her she probably won't get them back. Ask her if she'll make that contribution to the Moeller Athletic Department." He instructed a student manager to round up "the six best balls we've got" and take them to the game. Each team supplies its own game balls on offense, and Gerry did not want to go a whole game with two that had become waterlogged after one quarter. "We're going to spray the bottoms of everyone's shoes," he announced. He had found a product that keeps mud from sticking to the soles of football shoes.

The night's opponent had dominated Cincinnati football for most of the 1960s and inflicted the worst beating any Moeller team ever experienced, back in 1967. Though Gerry said "I forgot about that score the next year," Moeller had avenged that humiliation convincingly and completely. In the decade of the 1970s, Moeller outscored the Spartans, 284–8.

It is Gerry's stated belief that every player is on his team for a reason, whether he plays all the time or hardly at all. With Moeller's eighth straight league championship dangling in the downpour, it was Bob Hill's turn to contribute. Bob Hill was mistakenly called a tight end. Actually, he was a loose end—very loose. He played seldom, primarily because he was a junior behind two seniors. But he was the team comedian, specializing in impersonations including a pretty good Gerry Faust. By game time it had been raining for two hours. The field was barely playable and conditions were not going to improve. The game was postponed until 1 o'clock the next afternoon. Bob Hill's teammates were frustrated, primed for nothing after a day of disruption.

"Hill!" Gerry shouted in the crowded stadium locker room. A head popped up from the far corner. "Get up here!"

For the next 15 minutes, Bob Hill took requests and mimicked half the coaching staff, several teachers, and a few teammates to the hooting, howling, whistling approval of the whole squad. He had opened the valve, and a game's worth of steam was whooshing out.

Even with Bob Hill's help, it was difficult to recapture Friday night's intensity on Saturday afternoon. Moeller shut out Roger Bacon for the ninth year in a row, but a field goal was the only score of the first half. Two fourth-quarter touchdowns finally clinched Moeller's twelfth league title in 18 varsity seasons. Gerry made sure Bob Hill got into the game in the final two minutes.

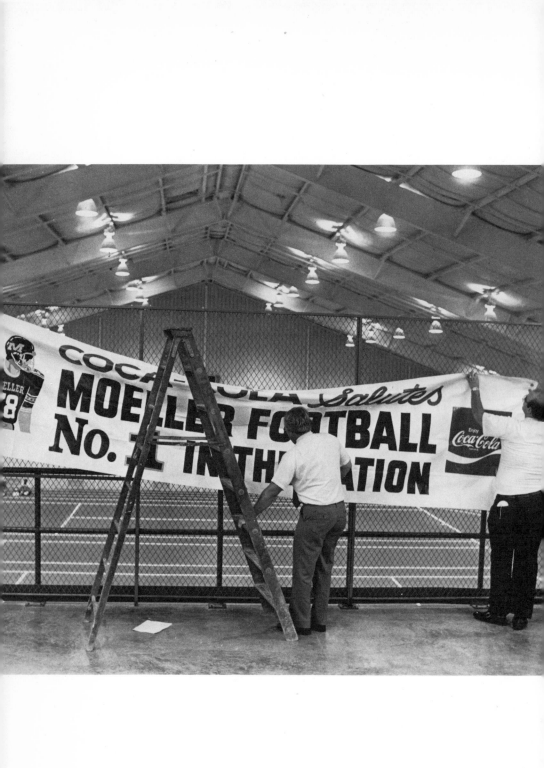

The Henry Gallenstein, Jr., Activity Center is lined off for the use of the tennis and track teams. Football players in foreground are practicing a few ballet steps, part of the quickness training incorporated into the Moeller football program. *Photo by Michael E. Keating.*

Moeller players were reminded of their heritage — self-discipline and excellence — every time they entered the locker room. *Photo by Ed Reinke.*

Gerry led the team onto the field for many years until his legs would not let him risk running in front of that thundering herd. *Moeller High School photo.*

Tim Koegel (14) was the only quarterback to start for Moeller for three seasons. From 1974 to 1976 Moeller won 33 and lost 1 in the games Koegel played. During his last year at Notre Dame, Koegel was reunited with his former coach. *Moeller High School photo.*

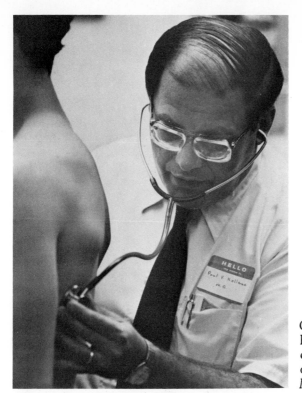

Cincinnati physician Paul V. Kollman helps with medical examinations on the first day of practice. *Photo by Michael E. Keating.*

The late John McDonald, first president of the Booster Club and one of Gerry's treasured senior-citizen volunteers. *Moeller High School photo.*

Tiny Tony Melink attempts a field goal for Moeller. *Moeller High School photo.*

Symbolic of Moeller football, the team helmet has been worn by 300 players who went on to college teams. *Moeller High School photo.*

Eric Ellington was Moeller's all-time leading ground gainer until the 1980 season when his record was broken by Mark Brooks. *Moeller High School photo*.

Steve Niehaus, another Moeller alumnus, was an All-American defensive lineman at Notre Dame and the first player drafted by the Seattle Seahawks.

Moeller grad Steve Sylvester played on two Super Bowl champions with the Oakland Raiders in 1977 and 1981.

Mark Brooks, who set numerous records during the 1980 season, will play for Faust at Notre Dame. *Moeller High School photo.*

Gerry wore his lucky hat only during state playoff games, and it never let him down. *Moeller High School photo.*

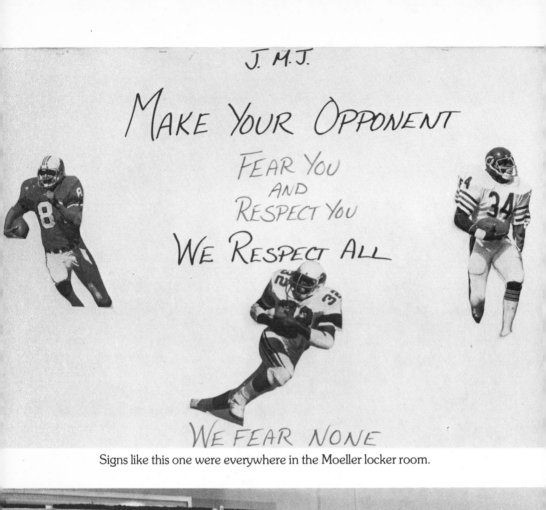

Signs like this one were everywhere in the Moeller locker room.

Gerry addresses the media at a press conference in South Bend after being named head coach at Notre Dame University. On the platform that day were (from left) former head coach Dan Devine; the Rev. Edmund P. Joyce, C.S.C., executive vice president of the University of Notre Dame; Gerry Faust; athletic director Gene Corrigan; and athletic director emeritus Edward W. "Moose" Krause. *Photo courtesy of the Notre Dame Sports Information Department.*

9

'I'd Never Date a Coach'

Marlene and Mary Ann, secretaries in the same office, were chatting one Monday morning in the spring of 1963. Excitedly, Mary Ann reviewed her weekend.

"I met this really neat guy! He's a football coach at Moeller."

"A football coach! I wouldn't even go out with him," said Marlene. "If he's a school teacher, he's never going to make any money . . . And if he's a coach, he'll be gone a lot. You're wasting your time. I'd *never* date a coach or a teacher. . . . "

Spring turned into summer, and summer to fall. On the second weekend of the football season Moeller's first senior team was humbled 32–6 by Cincinnati's resident powerhouse, Roger Bacon. The new school's young coach, who shared a house with seven fun-loving bachelors, went home to meditate on the defeat in the privacy of his own darkened bedroom. But Tex and George and Phil had other ideas.

"C'mon, you're going with us to a party."

"I'm not going anywhere."

"Sure you are."

"Leave me alone. I don't want to go anywhere."

They pulled him out of bed and he said, "I'm *not* going!" But by then he already had been dragged from his room and was being forcibly assisted down the steps.

Marlene the secretary was there when Gerry the coach arrived. He spotted her over in a corner, talking to a guy he did not know.

She was a nice-looking girl, he thought, dark-haired and petite. He decided to introduce himself. They chatted for a while; she had barely heard of Moeller, had no idea where it was located, and did not seem particularly anxious to learn more. When her girl friends wanted to leave, he walked her to their car. For the moment, he forgot about the bad second and third quarters against Bacon earlier that night. Moeller's edge in first downs but deficit in points ceased to haunt him. She really had not said anything to encourage him, but he was interested nonetheless.

Marlene was living with her sister at the time, and she had a steady boyfriend who had begun to window shop for an engagement ring. Gerry got her phone number from another girl at the party and happened to call when Marlene's suitor was out of town. She tried to decline politely, but he, fumbling for words, persisted awkwardly.

"I'm going with someone else," she said.

"Well, if you want to go out . . . you know, I mean, we can just go out with friends and have a good time . . . I mean, I'd be glad to take you out."

"I'm going with someone else," she said again.

"Well, I don't have that much time to date, because it's football season, you know, and I'm a coach. But I'd really like to take you out, you know, just to have a good time."

Gerry prolonged the conversation until she finally gave in. She was not sure why. Maybe it was the sincerity in his voice. Maybe it was his persistence. Maybe he just sounded like a nice guy. Whatever, she agreed to a movie. He called again, and she went out with him again. All of a sudden, at age 28, Gerry was falling in love.

It had been only five weeks since he introduced himself to her. Moeller had reeled off four straight victories and was getting ready for St. Xavier. It was a Sunday afternoon game, so there was time on Saturday night for a date. He was unprepared for her news flash when he called from the coaches' office that afternoon.

"I'm getting married," she told him. For a moment he could not hear everything she was saying. Her boyfriend had come back to town . . . He surprised her with a ring . . . Gerry was a really nice guy and she'd had fun going out with him, but she tried to tell him how things were the first time he called . . .

"I'm sure not very happy about this," he said. Boy, what an understatement! "But if that's your decision, all right. Fine. I wish you good luck."

As soon as he hung up the phone, Gerry headed for the courtyard at Moeller. He needed Mary's help. Once before he had met a girl he liked a lot. He had prayed to the Blessed Mother that time, too. He had prayed that he would marry the girl, but he also prayed that whenever he married, if ever he did, he would marry "a good Catholic girl" and they would have a big family and do a good job of raising the kids. When he did not marry the girl of his prayers, he told himself it was God's way of telling him it was not the right thing.

"Sometimes you have to wait for God to show you His plan," he told himself.

When he met Marlene, he was sure his prayer had been answered. He was sure the reason he did not marry his earlier love was because Marlene was the right girl for him. She had to be the answer to his prayers. As he stood before the statue, he was sure.

"Dear Mary," he prayed, "whatever your will is, is fine with me. I'll try to accept it. But I need your help. I'm really shook up. I really, really thought a lot of her." He paused, and then began: "Remember, O most gracious Virgin Mary . . ."

Across town, meanwhile, Marlene had gone to see a very close friend, a priest. She did not know what to do. She thought she wanted to marry this one guy, and then this other one came along and made her wonder. She was confused. She had doubts. She wanted his advice. They talked for a long time.

"You have to make your own decision," he told her. "But listening to you, I think you already have made up your mind."

Gerry went to a college game with a bunch of guys that night, but he was not himself—no jokes, no laughter, no pranks. They wanted to know why. He told them the whole story and, when the game was over, went home. Moeller still had to play St. Xavier the next afternoon. Gerry didn't know it, but one of his buddies, Pete Gray, had decided to call Marlene.

That Sunday was a beautiful day. The game attracted a large crowd, more than 3,500 fans. St. X scored first, and Moeller had a difficult time controlling the Bombers' line. The pass plays Gerry called were largely unsuccessful, but he found ways to run the ball. Moeller won 26–6, five straight and six-and-one on the season. When Pete Gray walked up to congratulate Gerry, he was accompanied by Gerry's newest fan.

"What are *you* doing here!" Gerry exclaimed.

"I came to see you coach the team," Marlene said. She had

decided to wait on engagement and marriage. She wanted to date Gerry for a while.

Being courted by Gerry was not a girl's basic romantic dream come true. He was not a bit pretentious. When he did not have a friend pick up Marlene for him, he would show up in his old car, wearing the most awful clothes she ever had seen. It was not his nature to be gentle or tender; he was rough even in those soft moments when the lights were low. Dates were football games until the season ended, and then basketball games. A movie was an exception. Usually they would go to a party afterward, and always the routine was the same. Gerry would go off and talk football, and come back when it was time to go home. Dinner out was at Gerry's favorite greasy spoon. They did not eat at a nice restaurant until after they were married. They visited his parents in Dayton quite often, too, and that is really what convinced Marlene she had found the right man.

"The thing that impressed me most about him was how he treated other people. You know, he's always been very kind and considerate of other people, especially his parents. When we would go up to Dayton and visit with them, he was always so kind and loving. That really impressed me because not many people are that way, when somebody else is around. But it just didn't make any difference who was there. I dated many, many guys, and had been to many houses, and nobody had ever done that. I thought, 'Gee, if he does that for his parents, he's going to be that way with his family.' "

Gerry and Marlene were married in April 1964, about eight months after they met. He proposed late one night, at Moeller of course. Brother Eveslage, the principal, was asleep in his room in the faculty residence wing when noise from the courtyard awakened him. He peered out his window, searching for the man whose voice he heard. There, in front of the Blessed Mother, stood Gerry with the woman he wanted to be his wife. Marlene Agruso, the secretary who said she never would date a coach, had just agreed to marry one.

The first year of marriage was not easy for Marlene. Gerry would tell his bride he would be home for dinner at 6, and she would rush home from work so she could have everything ready when he came through the door. Then she would wait and simmer, and eventually boil over as the pork chops languished in the skillet.

Gerry would come home, finally, around 8, and all through dinner he would talk on the phone. More than once that first year Marlene thought to herself:

"Gee, what did I get into? This is just not worth it. I could have stayed single."

As many men who teach school in the Cincinnati area have done for decades, Gerry worked summers at River Downs, the local horse track. Gerry has few vices. He does not smoke, and the only time he ever drank alcohol was when his buddies spiked his soft drink with vodka and he jumped off a diving board fully dressed at the Wright Patterson Air Force Base Officers' Club. He never uses profanity, either. "He's never said a bad word as long as we've been married," Marlene said after 17 years. "Honest to God, the guy's never—I have never heard him say one thing. In fact, when I get upset, I might, and then he gets upset with me. He just doesn't do it. He doesn't think it's necessary." But Gerry does enjoy a game of chance now and then. He could not work at the track and not bet on a few races. The result, to Marlene's distress, was that he worked the summer for virtually nothing.

"You'll have to quit your job," she told Gerry. "We're not making anything."

Through it all, Marlene tried hard to be a good wife. When Gerry would bring players home with him, as he often did, she would let them spend the night, if that is what he wanted. And she would feed them, even though she really did not know what football players ate. Once that first year he brought one of his starters home on a Friday afternoon. The game was that night. In those days Catholics did not eat meat on Fridays, so Marlene whipped up a tuna casserole. She encouraged a second helping, and a third, too. The boy really seemed to enjoy it, which pleased her. She was proud of herself. She did not know you do not stuff a football player hours before he goes out to block and tackle. The lad turned a little green with the first few hits and sat out most of the game. On later occasions Marlene searched her recipe file for lighter Friday fare.

The only time she was really annoyed by Gerry's habit of bringing home strays for dinner was after they had started a family and he would call at the last minute. She had the babies to feed, and dinner for two was already on the stove. On his end of the phone, with a friend at his side, Gerry would cheerfully announce he was bringing someone home for dinner. On her end she would be yelling at him. What was she supposed to feed the guy? Once she served the visitor her own portion, made excuses for not joining them, and sat down to a TV dinner by herself. She would wonder, "What did I get into?" But Gerry would always come through with a thank-you note.

Gerry was eager to have a family, and Julie, their first born, came along rather quickly. Since motherhood was a new experience for Marlene at the age of 26, she stayed with her parents for the first few weeks. Gerry visited daily but continued to sleep and eat at their apartment. The day he brought Marlene and Julie home was indeed a memorable occasion.

"Would you care if I go out and play poker tonight?" he said.

"You've got to be kidding!"

"Well, I promised these other coaches that I would."

"After two weeks?"

"Well, I promised."

"Oh! You promised! In that case, go! Don't break your promise."

So Gerry played poker. And Marlene sat home alone with her new baby, angry, hurt, disappointed. When Julie started crying later in the evening, she called the poker game.

"Come home and take care of your daughter. She's crying."

He was furious with her for calling. She was even madder at him for leaving in the first place. He came home. It was the low point of their marriage, though short-lived.

Four years married and four times pregnant, Marlene followed Julie with a miscarriage, then a son, Gerry, and another son, Steve. An older couple in the neighboring apartment took a liking to the young mother with three little ones. The man would often take Julie and young Gerry for a walk while the wife gave Marlene a hand with Stevie. That helped a lot. And her best friend, Jan Schneider, and Jan's husband Ken, an attorney who provided legal services to the Moeller Boosters Club and became Gerry's lawyer, came over whenever Marlene asked. Marlene was thankful, too, for the support and advice of her mother, who several years later came to live with them and often told Marlene: "You'll never find anybody as good as he is. There aren't too many men like him."

But mostly, Marlene coped on her own. "I've got all these kids," she told herself, "and he's not going to be around to help me. If I'm going to stay married and be happy, I'm going to have to adjust. I'm going to have to change, because he's not going to."

Marlene learned to live with Gerry's idiosyncrasies and appreciate his sincerity, generosity, and genius. She became a football fan, a Moeller fan—a Gerry Faust fan. During the first five years of their marriage, Gerry could not sleep the night before a game. He would pace the floor all night, and she would stay awake with him, to talk or listen or just be there if he needed her. Moeller lost nine games and tied two in those five years. To each defeat Gerry responded with prolonged silence and an intense self-examination to determine what he had done wrong and how he could prevent the same mistake in the future. Marlene endured with patience and understanding. Through the years she earned her husband's complete admiration.

"I don't think I could be married to a better person," he has said often. "I don't think there's another woman who could put up with what she puts up with. The hours I'm gone, the type of person I am—I'm not an easy person to live with, you know. But she's just great about it. I really call her a saint. She's a great mother and a great wife and a great example to the kids. Over the years our marriage has gotten better. A lot of people feel they start out real good, and then they go the other way. Ours started out rotten. You've really got to give her credit. It's unbelievable how she handled it."

While Gerry did everything at Moeller, he did nothing at home. Marlene reared the children and provided most of the discipline; kept the checkbook and paid all the bills; and, if something needed fixing, fixed it herself or hired someone to do the job. When Gerry came home, it was to eat, sleep, talk on the phone, watch a sports event, or share time with Marlene and the children. Sunday nights were reserved for the family, and he always stopped for a two-week vacation in July before summer practice began. The rest of the time he was coaching, scouting, raising money, attending meetings, planning for next year, working with college recruiters, or making speeches. As so many people have discovered, Marlene became convinced that the quality of time spent together is more important than the quantity.

"I have a lot of friends who are divorced because of a situation where the man was around a lot, but he really wasn't. You know, they can be around a lot but still not give themselves to you. Gerry's not around a lot, but when he's around, he's with us. And when he's really needed, he's there. He's never really that far away."

For providing Moeller High School with the nation's most

remarkable high school football program Gerry was paid $1,550. The rest of his Moeller paycheck was basic faculty salary in the high teens and another $2,170 for serving as athletic director. With his speaking fees and other sidelines, though, he was able to provide a $135,000 house in one of Cincinnati's finer neighborhoods and support an affluent lifestyle that included designer clothes, movie screen television, and private school tuition of $1,200 a year for Julie. Gerry's Christmas presents to Marlene their last few years in Cincinnati were fabulous—a new car, a diamond ring, a color television. The Fausts lived very well in the later years of Gerry's 20-year career at Moeller. "He wasn't an ordinary high school coach," Marlene smiled.

Not surprisingly, Moeller was the center of the family life. The family room where the Fausts spent their most time together was a shrine to the success of the man of the house. The plaques, trophies, proclamations, and acclamations framed and displayed in that room numbered more than fifty. "And I have three or four times that many packed away in boxes," Marlene said.

There was a plaque on the wall for Marlene, too. It is the front half of a wine bottle, presented to her by friends who rode the booster bus the day they plied her with wine from start to finish on a three-hour ride to Findlay, Ohio. A reserved personality, Marlene Faust had no idea what they were doing to her until it was too late. "By the time we got there she was ready to go down in the locker room and help the boys get dressed," relished Hank Leeseman, a fervent Moeller booster who delighted in recounting the story loudly enough for Marlene to hear even in a noisy crowd. Marlene was embarrassed by it all and was reluctant to hang the plaque. But the people who joke with you the most are usually the people who like you best. Moeller boosters were a part of her family, too.

Marlene missed only two games in 17 years, once when she was pregnant and once when she was ill. She became the adviser for the cheerleaders, who came together from three girls academies on the Moeller side of town. Julie was a junior varsity cheerleader when they moved to South Bend. The Faust boys had virtually free run of the locker room, coaches' office, practice field, and sideline. They rode the team bus to almost every game; the travel time was an opportunity for their dad to spend a few minutes talking and joking with them.

Gerry did not spend the kind of time he wanted with his boys, because he spent so much with other men's sons. At best he would catch a few quarters of their whole football season, a few innings of baseball all summer. He would excuse his coaches from meetings so they could attend their sons' games, but he did not feel he could excuse himself. Like most fathers who miss seeing their children grow up, Gerry thought about it often. It bothered him. "I think they understand," he said. "I hope they understand. I hope they know I really love them."

He had his own ways of showing them. Every night when he arrived home, no matter the time, he gave each one a hug and a kiss and told them: "I love you." If they woke up and felt it even half the time, it was often enough. He kept a statue of a saint in each child's room and prayed to each one to protect that child. He would wake them in the morning, just before he left for school, so he could say hello and goodbye and see them awake for a moment. His relationship with Julie, Gerry, and Steve may not have been a traditional one, but it was predictable and consistent. They understood.

Julie wrote a paper on her father once. It said everything Gerry could ever have hoped such a composition would say:

> I am very proud of my dad and I love him very much. When my dad wins his games I am even more proud of him because I think he deserves to win because of all the work he puts in. He really loves football and I'm glad that he enjoys it because that makes me enjoy it even more. I go to every game because I enjoy watching my dad and the team win. Also, if I didn't go I know that it would upset him and I wouldn't want to hurt his feelings because it means a lot to him for us to be there. I would say we are a very close family. The time that my dad doesn't spend with us, he makes up for. He is always there whenever we need him for anything. I wouldn't know what I would do without him. I think he is the most generous person in the world, and I'm not saying this just because he is my dad. It's because it's the truth. When people ask me what it's like to have a famous father, I tell them it isn't different from their own father. People also ask me if he treats us like he treats the football players, and I tell them: No. He is completely the opposite. He is really a softy.

In their seventh and eighth grade years, Julie's brothers seemed to be following their father's every footstep. Gerry and

Steve played football, basketball, and baseball with the same distinction as their father at that age. They did not seem destined for stardom as Moeller football players, but Marlene and Gerry agreed that the boys deserved the opportunity to be on Moeller's team if they wanted to work at it, whether they played or not. The unhappiest prospect of the Notre Dame opportunity for Gerry was leaving Moeller before his sons could attend the school. He was looking forward to four years with each one.

Seeing his sons grow up to be football stars or great coaches was not important to Gerry. Only one thing mattered as he watched his little girl become a young woman and his little boys become men.

"I really mean this from the bottom of my heart," he said. "I don't care what sports they play, or what they do in life. That's their decision and I'm behind them all the way. The only thing I want them to do is try to be good in life. I always tell them that. I say, 'As long as you try to be a good person, I'll be the proudest father in the world.' "

THE END OF AN ERA

GAME NINE: MOELLER vs. AKRON WALSH JESUIT

October 25, 1980

The most important special occasion during the Moeller football season was Moms & Dads Night. It was even bigger than Homecoming or Advertisers' Night. The parents of the senior players were invited to accompany their sons through the entire pregame ritual. They crowded into the chapel for Benediction; they jammed the locker room for the pep talks; and before the game each mother and father greeted their boy at the 50-yard line and he kissed them. "Parents," Gerry warned, "if you don't kiss him back, your boy won't play."

Gerry always told coaching clinic audiences he felt a coach should know every player's home environment. "We have two hundred and ten players," he said, "and I know every kid and their home situation—if there's an alcoholic in the family, if there has been a death, or any other possible problem. It is important to know this because you can't deal with a boy unless you know his environment." When confronted with separated parents on Moms & Dads Night, Gerry would telephone them individually and ask them if they could spend five minutes together for the sake of their son. "I tell them their boy is more important than their differences. I tell them it is important for that kid to have his parents there. I tell them that for five minutes they can do it. I have never had a parent turn me down. I have had parents who went out there and did not speak to each other, but they came. We have never had a problem."

It was no coincidence that Gerry scheduled this emotional evening for the ninth game of the season, the one immediately preceding the Princeton game. Princeton was the only Cincinnati team to beat Moeller in seven years; the game was always a tense, close one; and since the start of football playoffs in 1972 it had always determined the representative from southwestern Ohio. Moms & Dads Night was the perfect antidote to that irresistible temptation to look ahead a week to the waiting Princeton Vikings. With more than 50 proud mothers and fathers standing elbow to elbow in the locker room amid their padded, helmeted sons, Gerry called the roll of coaches as usual and their comments flowed in a stream of consciousness that passed smoothly from one man to another.

"Your parents have done an awful lot for you, but until you get into your thirties you don't appreciate them the way you should," Steve Klonne began. "I don't think there's any greater compliment you can give your parents than to reach down inside yourselves tonight and play your best game," Jim Higgins continued. "A lot of sacrifices have been made for you. Take a couple of minutes to think about what life is all about," said Mike Cameron. "We take this for granted, but this is an exciting moment for them," Paul Smith pointed out. "We talk about how hard summer practice is and how much sacrifice we put into our season—it's not all fun and games for them, either."

With Mr. Bachi waiting in the coaches' office, Ted Bacigalupo added another thought. "We're always talking about the Moeller family. It's great to have the rest of the family here tonight." And then Pat Orloff said, "I know what your parents are feeling tonight. I've got kids your age! And I know what it means to have parents who are interested in you. My dad never missed a game when I played." The last man called on to speak was Bill Clark, who had coached his own son during his many years with Gerry. "I've been on both sides, as a coach and a parent. All you can consider is how lucky you are that you have parents who are here, who care about you, who love you," Bill said. "My parents were separated. I didn't see my father, and he never saw me play."

Gerry spoke the final words and chose to lighten the moment a little. "You guys," he said to the seniors, "take your helmets off when you kiss your parents."

Walsh Jesuit had won seven and lost only one and was a state playoffs contender in its own region. The Warriors' only loss was to an unbeaten team from suburban Akron. Several hundred fans made the four-and-a-half-hour trip from Akron, many bringing with them miniature cowbells that had become a trademark of the Walsh cheering section. Moeller won the coin toss and Gerry took the wind advantage, which meant he was willing to give the visitors possession of the ball to start the game and again to open the second half. Not many high school coaches can afford to make decisions based on which way the wind blows, but it took Moeller only four minutes to turn that decision into six points. The Moeller defense forced a punt into that wind and the kick was returned to the Walsh 23-yard line. Mark Brooks tied a school record for career scoring a few plays later on a three-yard run.

It was 21–0 by halftime, when the senior members of Moeller's first state champion football team, the 1975 squad, were honored. For the occasion Gerry bought them all special T-shirts with the lettering: 1975 State Champions Moeller High School. Introduced individually, they ran onto the field with arms waving. They jumped up and down and roughhoused with each other as though they were in uniform and about to answer a kickoff themselves.

"Those guys made all of this possible," freshman coach Ted Hall said as he watched them. "We had lost in the first round of the playoffs two years in a row, and people were beginning to wonder if Moeller could go all the way. These guys did it. I don't think many of them could have started on this year's team, or on either of the last two state champions. Our kids now are so much more advanced; they have so much more natural ability. But those guys had tremendous heart. They came from behind in seven games that year. They started what we have going now."

Gerry expressed similar sentiments in the locker room and sent the 1980 Moeller Crusaders back to the field with instructions to follow the example of the 1975 Moeller Crusaders. Moms & Dads Night concluded as a 42–0 success. Every senior played in front of his parents. Before the end of the third quarter, starters were leaving the game, replaced by second-teamers. Also before the end of the third quarter, a few folks in the crowd were fleeing the unseasonably cold temperatures. The windchill factor was 28 degrees below zero at game time.

Even Gerry allowed his attention to wander from the field for a few moments. He trotted to the fence separating the field from the stadium stands, reached across to a man and woman about to leave, and hugged them both. As he gave each one a kiss, he said: "Goodnight, Mom. Goodnight, Dad. I love you."

10

Great Friends of Moeller

They were doctors, lawyers, bankers, builders, painters, plumbers, salesmen, and businessmen. Many were housewives. One was a professional dance instructor. There were hundreds of them, and Gerry called each one "A Great Friend Of Moeller." Certainly Moeller football could not have been what it was under Gerry without their help. In one decade they raised hundreds of thousands of dollars, published the largest program-lineup magazine ever sold at a high school football game, and built a million-dollar building. They did whatever Gerry asked—even when it meant driving to a testing lab at 6 in the morning to shave for the financial benefit of Moeller athletics—and never questioned his use of the resources they provided.

No price can be placed on the vast amount of time and labor this army of supporters donated to the Moeller cause. In pure dollars and cents, the boosters provided almost half of the $125,000 Moeller spent on athletics each year. The home game program, which required the operational and organizational equivalent of a small company, generated almost $30,000 in advertising revenue alone. Almost that much more came from meat sales, dances, product testing, and other activities throughout the year.

The 200-page 1980 program contained 282 ads, weighed three pounds, and brought in more money than many high schools realize from a whole season of football gate receipts. The book represented the collective efforts of more than a hundred boosters and Moeller faculty members, coordinated by Gerry and two close friends, Don and Marge Hauser. Gerry and Don are the same age and, coincidentally, were pictured on the same newspaper sports page when they were high school football players, even though Gerry played for Chaminade in Dayton and Don for Central in Cincinnati. They first met years later.

Like most of the people who worked so hard for Gerry, the Hausers had a son who played for him. Danny Hauser was Moeller's quarterback for two seasons, 1970–71. The Moeller program book was born in 1970 with Don Hauser in charge, as he was a decade later. "It's really like a big family," Hauser said of working with the Moeller boosters. "When the kids leave, most of the parents stay with the program."

Indeed, the Hausers were not alone in longevity. Ted Gramman's boy, Denny, was the starting fullback and a captain in 1972 and signed with Alabama; Ted kept the boosters' books for more than 10 years. Greg Storer was a high school All-American in 1974 and played for Ohio State; his parents continued to send out the bills to advertisers and keep payments straight six years after their son graduated from Moeller. Between 1968 and 1976 the Koegels cheered three sons at Moeller: linebacker Vic and offensive guard Steve, who both attended Ohio State, and quarterback Tim, who was still at Notre Dame when Gerry arrived; in 1980 the Koegels were still in charge of Booster Club membership and the boosters' monthly meat sale. And John Hatfield, who suggested a swim party and cookout for the seniors when his first son played in 1968, was still welcoming the seniors into his backyard 13 years later.

Doctors whose sons attended Moeller stayed with Gerry and the football program long after their boys had moved on to college and adulthood. Physical examinations on the opening day of summer practice involved an ever-increasing number of physician volunteers, 24 in 1980. There were ear, nose, and throat specialists; orthopedic surgeons; cardiologists; radiologists; podiatrists; urologists; and even a vascular surgeon. In one hour's time each boy visited them all.

Such a healthy screening would cost "several thousand dollars," estimated Dr. Hank Cianciolo, "but none of the guys charge for this." Doc Cianciolo was director of the Family Practice Program at the University of Cincinnati Medical Center and a Moeller team doctor when they could be counted on one hand. "Most of the guys have had sons attend Moeller at some time," he said, "and the rest are in practice with them." At least one doctor visited Moeller during or after practice every day of the season.

Gerry also found retirees a ready resource just waiting to help. John McDonald, the first president of the boosters, and Harry Becker, whose daughter married Phil Gigliotti, one of Gerry's closest friends and one of his assistants for 16 years, were both handy with tools. Logically, they became Moeller's equipment managers and athletic department handymen. Bob Bacigalupo (Mr Bachi) and Art Gormley, who were good at counting money and keeping records, were perfect as Moeller's ticket managers.

Justifiably, Gerry raved about "our senior citizens" everywhere he went. It was a fantastic exchange. High school boys learned to respect and appreciate the wisdom and knowledge that comes with age, and these men experienced the contagious vibrance of youth and the pleasure of good company. Gerry had complimented them by recognizing the valuable contribution they could make in retirement, and they responded with outstanding performance.

It was impossible to repay everyone for their time and effort, but Gerry tried. Each June he spent $5,000 on a Moeller family outing, the annual corn roast. Bus driver Carl Rahe and his family would do the cooking—300 steaks and 500 ears of corn. The food was free, the drinks were free, and Gerry bought little favors for everyone—glasses imprinted with "Moeller No. 1."

The boosters celebrated together at the end of each season, too. Seven hundred and fifty people paid $2.50 apiece to sit through a five-hour awards banquet at which no food was served. Some would bring their own trays of hors d'oeuvres to go with the free soft drinks; it evolved into a very popular party. Bob and Joan Maegly, whose only son, Tim, played *basketball* not football, crafted handmade mementos for all of the senior football players for more than a decade, and Gerry spent a thousand dollars on other awards; practically everyone associated with the football program received something.

Films of the previous weekend's game were reviewed each Monday night of the season, attracting an audience of as many as 150 faithful—mostly parents. It was at one such film session that the unique idea of ballet lessons for football players arose. As one dimensional as Gerry may seem, he has a latent appreciation for art, music, and dance. "Your best athlete is either a gymnast or a dancer," he says. "You coordinate something different each time in dancing." Gerry told the boosters he hoped to start a dance program, specifically ballet, if he could find a qualified "coach" to work with the players. He was sure it would help the quickness and agility of the Moeller linemen.

The following morning Betty Behm, the mother of two of Gerry's players, called with a name. Choreographer Jack Louiso, whose only sport in high school had been golf, was accepting private students. Louiso had been the choreographer for the Cincinnati Summer Opera for 11 years and had similar credits with opera companies in Tulsa, Seattle, and Hawaii. Gerry contacted him immediately and received a cool reception.

"I'm busy creating professional dancers," Louiso said.

Gerry persisted, of course, and prevailed.

"Not until he made it clear they might go on professionally—as football players—did I change my attitude," Louiso explained in 1974, the first year of classes. "I'm interested that these guys might be able to go on and play college or pro football because of this training."

Ten linemen made up the Moeller football team's first ballet class. They were embarrassed and hated the thought of it. All the jokes from their buddies at school did not help. And the giggly little girls in the class ahead of theirs only made it worse. The darlings always stayed and watched.

"They came out and called us sissies," groaned red-haired Jeff Hock, a six-foot-three, 220-pound tackle, whose father ranks as one of Moeller's most generous boosters. "They want to know if we can do the splits."

But the boys had no choice. Gerry told them they would not play football at Moeller unless they attended ballet lessons. "Hut-hut-hut" was replaced in their vocabulary with "Step, step-step, back, step; turn, two-three-four; cross, cross, back-together; jump side, jump back, jump side, jump front, jump all the way around . . ." It was Knute Rockne and The Four Horsemen all over again—without piano accompaniment.

Louiso quickly came to enjoy the classes. The boys were good kids who were never tardy or absent and who always made a sincere effort to follow his instructions. Things began looking up for the boys, as well. The ballerinas became their friends, and the guys at school were silenced by a few demonstrations. Quickness tests showed the boys were making noticeable improvement in their speed and lateral movement.

"It was unbelievable," Gerry told coaches at clinics. "Jim Donnellon, one of our offensive tackles that year, would *not* have played for me without the improvement he made in ballet. He went on to Wittenberg College, started for three years, and played on a national champion."

By 1980 Gerry had 100 football players pirouetting in the off-season, 50 in advanced and 50 in beginning classes. And there was a waiting list. After the final class each spring, Jack Louiso would predict the next season's starters based solely on their performance in ballet. He was right 80 percent of the time. Intrigued with the innovation, Woody Hayes once approached Louiso about teaching ballet to Ohio State linemen.

"I only work for one coach," Louiso said.

The willingness—the eagerness—of so many people to help Gerry in so many ways was a comment on the man himself. Success and fame attract hangers-on; sincerity attracts workers.

"Gerry Faust is the kind of guy who could call you in the middle of the night to tell you he'd run out of gas, and you'd be in such a hurry to help him that you'd hang up and leave the house before you found out *where* he left his car," said Fran Dugan. "He's the kind of guy you want to do things for. He's so unselfish and so appreciative and so enthusiastic. He makes you *want* to help him! He has more of that quality than anyone I've ever known."

Fran Dugan is president of Dugan & Meyers, a construction company doing business in five states. He will be remembered as the man who built Gerry's dream building by committing his company to $150,000 worth of work without a guarantee of payment, calling in favors from long-time suppliers, and persuading friends to price at cost or donate another $200,000 worth of materials and labor. The result was a structure officially named the Henry Gallenstein, Jr., Activity Center (always referred to by Gerry as simply "the new addition").

The activity center, situated 20 feet behind the gym at Moeller, is a monument to all who responded to Gerry so generously during his two decades at the high school. It is a big building, 24,000 square feet on the ground floor and 8,000 square feet on the mezzanine. It houses two indoor tennis courts, an indoor track, a three-mat wrestling room, and a baseball batting cage. There is room for two classrooms, a band room, and a small theater. In bad weather the football team can hold a full practice indoors, and coaches who like an elevated vantage point can observe from the mezzanine level. The Moeller marching band also can practice its routines indoors when necessary.

"That building would never have been built without Fran Dugan," Gerry says. "Fran built it. An awful lot of people made tremendous contributions—some of them donated thousands of dollars worth of work or materials or equipment—but Fran brought it all together."

Dugan got to know Gerry when his oldest son enrolled at Moeller in 1972, but he did not attend the Monday night film meetings until his second son started playing for Gerry five years later. Dugan rarely missed a Moeller game, but he was too busy to become a rabid Moeller booster. "I don't volunteer for committees, and I don't join clubs or run for election to things like parish councils," he said. "I don't have the time. I have a profession and I'm happy to act as a consultant or take on a job in that field if anyone ever feels my knowledge and my skills can be of help. That's what I'm good at."

Gerry had started planning an all-purpose athletic building and praying for a way to pay for it in the early 1970s. The wrestling team was practicing in a classroom; the track team was running through the halls; and off-season quickness drills for the football team were being held in the cafeteria. All were taking their toll on the school building. Gerry asked a drafting teacher to draw sketches of a new gym, and for several years Gerry showed the drawings to various wealthy residents of the Moeller district in the hope that one or two would want to finance his dream. But that hope was a dream in itself. Despite Gerry's many prayers, no angels with bulging bank-rolls came forth. In 1978 he turned to Fran Dugan.

"He gave me his 'plans' with all his usual enthusiasm," Dugan recalled. "He wanted to know what it would cost."

Gerry was thinking $300,000.

"Somewhere around nine hundred thousand," Dugan estimated. Gerry was speechless. Dugan told him he never would get his building built if he continued to look for one benefactor. "You need a lot of people with a hundred dollars each," he advised.

Dugan had done some work for the Archdiocese of Cincinnati when his company was new and small; in fact, Dugan & Meyers had bid unsuccessfully on the Moeller High School construction job in 1958. Recalling a lesson the Catholic Church taught him early in his career, Dugan told Gerry:

"The thing to do is to raise enough money to get started. It's always easier to raise money for a building project after you have something coming out of the ground. That's the way they paid for half the churches in Cincinnati."

Dugan suggested major changes in the plans and told Gerry that Dugan & Meyers would carry part of the project for a while if he could raise enough money to get started. By then the first game of the 1978 season had become Moeller's thirty-seventh victory in a row. The next game would be tough enough without any distractions; the Princeton Vikings had proven repeatedly that they could compete with Moeller. Gerry was preoccupied all that week with organizing the Committee of 40 and getting the fund-raising effort underway. He had heard that another school in the area was planning a fund drive, too, and he wanted to be sure Moeller got a head start. He succeeded at that; during the month that followed the committee raised $225,000. But Moeller's winning streak was broken by Princeton. Gerry took a bad gamble late in a close game. A field goal with six seconds to play was the difference in a 13–12 defeat. He moped for weeks and blamed himself for putting the building fund ahead of a tough game.

The first phase of construction, completed in early 1980, carried a price tag of $650,000. The unpaid bill amounted to roughly one third of that. Faced with such a staggering debt, Gerry enlisted the aid of the president of one of Cincinnati's largest banks. Joe Rippe had connections; he knew how to raise money. He suggested that the "new addition" be named for Henry Gallenstein, a patron of countless charities and a man who was especially kind to projects benefitting young people. Rippe proposed a dinner party at his estate in Gallenstein's honor, with proceeds benefitting the Moeller building fund. Tickets sold for $500 a couple. Almost 800 people attended.

When Gerry left Moeller for Notre Dame the Henry Gallenstein, Jr., Activity Center was not yet complete. Another $200,000 worth of work on the classrooms, band room-theater, and shower areas was planned in two phases. The drive to finish "the new addition" began, appropriately, with a "Gerry Faust Roast."

THE END OF AN ERA

GAME TEN: MOELLER vs. PRINCETON

October 31, 1980

Pat Mancuso, Princeton High School's football coach and athletic director, is unlike Gerry in every way but record. He is a measured, thoughtful man not given to bursts of impulse or flamboyance, a dapper fellow of polished manner. His black hair is always coiffed, his shoes always polished, and his clothes always pressed and the colors coordinated. Even the bermuda shorts he wears to practice are stylish. Mancuso's first year at Princeton, a huge public school with a coed enrollment of 2,800 students in three grades, was also Gerry's first year at Moeller. They started playing each other in Moeller's third varsity season, and it quickly became Cincinnati's most intense rivalry. Princeton won only three times in 15 years, but 11 times the winning team scored only two touchdowns. Typical scores were 13–12, 12–10, 14–6, 14–11, 12–9, and 13–6.

Though Mancuso's program at Princeton did not duplicate Gerry's, it was larger and more successful than any other school in southwestern Ohio. Princeton won or shared league championships 17 times in the first 20 years Mancuso was head coach. Under him the Vikings were state champions in 1978 and runners-up in 1972. His record for two decades at Princeton was 154 victories, 37 defeats, and 11 ties, a winning percentage of .806 compared to Gerry's .905.

Mancuso respected Gerry, although he disagreed with him. Like so many coaches in Cincinnati, he thought the Moeller football program had grown out of proportion. He thought Moeller had too many coaches. And while he did not believe illegal recruiting was taking place in 1980, he did believe the Moeller mystique was so far-reaching that it had the same effect. But he also recognized that Gerry worked harder than any other coach, and that Gerry's sacrifice and dedication were not to be denied. He never complained or criticized Gerry publicly, and when his coaches would start grousing, he would stop them cold.

"We don't *have* to play them," he emphasized. "We play them because we choose to play them. And that means we choose to play them knowing exactly what kind of program they have. The only schools that have any right to complain or criticize are the schools in their league. Those schools don't have a choice. They have to play them even if they don't want to, even if they disagree totally with the philosophy of the football program at Moeller."

Until 1980 the Moeller-Princeton game traditionally was played no later than the third week of the season. In the first eight years of the state playoffs, however, that early-season game had ultimately decided the region's playoff representative every year. Five times the winner of that game eventually won the state championship. Gerry thought it made sense to capitalize on the perennial importance of the game by making it the last one of the season. He envisioned both teams coming into the game unbeaten, with a trip to the playoffs the winner's prize. The 1980 season unfolded according to plan—up to the unbeaten part. Moeller and Princeton had each won nine straight when it came time to meet. But fate had turned this end-of-the-season showdown, this game for all the marbles, into a mere tuneup or preliminary for a more important game a week later. A regional round was added to the playoffs in 1980, and Princeton and Moeller had clinched those regional playoff berths with their ninth victories. They were going to play each other back to back—double jeopardy.

It is not unusual for two professional teams to play each other more than once in a season, and bowl games sometimes provide a rematch between college teams. But high school teams rarely play opponents more than once a season. It presented a fascinating strategical dilemma. Should a team hold back anything for the second game? Who would have the psychological advantage in the second game, the first game's winner or loser? Could either team beat the other two weeks in a row? The questions had never been considered before, much less answered.

"You blow them out the first time," declared Moeller's Jeff Leibert. "You don't hold anything back. Get it in their minds that you're a better football team than they are. Then, the first time you score in the second game, they begin to sink."

Steve Klonne, who started watching Princeton films before the ninth game against Akron Walsh Jesuit had been played, liked Princeton's position. "The advantage in the first game is definitely

Princeton's," he offered. "They don't have to show everything. They're already in the playoffs. They can afford to lose." The implication was that Moeller could not. But Moeller had its spot in the playoffs secured as well. What was the difference?

"They're not playing for a national championship," Paul Smith answered gravely.

There was a glint in Gerry's eyes as he entered the discussion. "At first, I didn't like the idea of playing them twice in a row. Now I'm starting to get excited about it. I think it will be an interesting challenge."

Although an unbeaten season, not to mention team pride, was at stake in the first game, Moeller needed a victory in the second game to repeat as state champion. "The second one is the only one that counts," Ted Bacigalupo shrugged.

Baci was right, of course. Nevertheless there was great fan interest in the first game. Gerry favored playing it at Nippert Stadium, but it was Princeton's home game. And Mancuso was determined to play on his home field even though Princeton Stadium, the best high school stadium in Cincinnati, had a seating capacity of 7,000 compared to Nippert's 27,000.

"It is a high school game and it belongs on the high school campus," Mancuso insisted. "We're not playing this game for the whole city; we're playing it for the students from the two schools. It's not a high school football game anymore when you take it away from the high school and play it in a college stadium."

Gerry disagreed. "He just wants to keep the game at Princeton because he thinks he has a better chance of beating us there," he said. "When winning becomes so important that you forget about the fans, I think there's something wrong. If people want to see the game, they ought to be able to buy a ticket; we could draw twenty-five thousand people to that game. And they ought to be able to get a seat. There'll be five thousand people standing at Princeton, and none of them will be able to see a thing."

It was exam week at both schools. No pep rallies are permitted at Moeller during exams, but Princeton was having one. When Gerry found out, he relished the opportunity to needle Mancuso during one of several phone conversations they had that week.

"See, athletics comes before academics at Princeton," he taunted with a big grin. "We can't get away with anything like that at Moeller. You *run* that school." Mancuso had a retort, then the call was over. "That's the loosest he's ever been," Gerry mused. "He really thinks he can beat us this year."

Roger Staubach visited Moeller in midweek. He appeared without fanfare to watch a freshman game; the son of an old friend was playing for Moeller. Few people realized he was there. Gerry knew, of course, and tapped him for some advice. Staubach faced some teams twice every season in the National Football League. They talked strategy, not psychology. Staubach's advice: Don't add plays for the second game; use the same plays but add some wrinkles. Change your pass patterns.

The last day of regular season practice at Moeller is called "Senior Day." Among the traditions, each understudy decorates his senior's shoes. Big Doug Williams, for example, was presented with hot-pink size-fourteens covered with feathers and big bows. Tim King's treads resembled a '56 Chevy with a bright, furry collar. And placekicker Tony Melink's pair were a shade of green that almost glowed in the dark. They were designed to catch everyone's eye on game night.

The regular season Moeller-Princeton game of 1980 was played on Halloween. The stadium was packed at 6:30; by 8 o'clock there were 7,000 people sitting and roughly 8,000 standing. Steve and Gerry Faust, the coach's sons, passed up the game to go trick-or-treating.

To Pat Mancuso there was no question about the importance of Game One. "We considered the first one the state championship game," he said a few weeks later. "We were the number one and two teams in the state. We were both unbeaten. One of us was going to lose the next week; there was no way we were going to meet with perfect records in the state championship game. That made our first game the state finals, as far as we were concerned." The game was played with championship intensity. "It was everything a high school game should be," he said.

The first half was a standoff, five Princeton punts and a bad punt snap, two Moeller fumbles, two Moeller passes intercepted, and a Moeller punt. Mike Willging passed eight yards to Ron Lindhorst for a Moeller touchdown with nine minutes to play in the second quarter. It remained 7–0 until the last 30 seconds of the half. Princeton's "Dangerous" David Keeling, quicksilver in shoulder pads, made five yards with a couple of sudden cuts and then picked up 65 more with his jackrabbit speed. It was tied. Gerry gambled and almost paid dearly in the few seconds that remained. A pass in the flat was intercepted on Moeller's 34-yard line. Pass interference against Moeller moved the ball to the 19 on the next play. With nine seconds on the clock, Princeton was within field goal range. The kick was wide.

The second half opened with each team punting. Then Moeller put together its first sustained drive. It began at the Moeller 13 and carried to the Princeton 47, eight plays, before it sputtered and another punt was in order. Keeling did it again, 74 yards this time, and Princeton had the lead, 13–7. Moeller was in trouble, but the snap on the extra point was mishandled, a very big play.

The final 16 minutes were the most dramatic, the most excruciating, of the entire Moeller season. The Moeller offense had not been able to hold the ball for more than nine consecutive plays all night; four penalties and four turnovers added up to an uncharacteristically sloppy performance. The time had come for perfection. The Crusaders started on their 30. Seventeen running plays later, Mark Brooks covered the last three feet on third-and-goal. Tony Melink could put Moeller ahead, 14–13, with an extra point kick.

The snap was low. Melink started into his stride, then stopped—with his leg already cocked. Holder Lindhorst, the ex-quarterback, was clutching for control of the spinning ball. He set it up a bit crooked; Princeton defenders were closing in. Melink pulled the trigger. His luminously shoed foot came forward in the motion of a nine-iron. The ball wobbled through the air. Kick good!

Aside from the 144 yards David Keeling had gained on two plays, the Moeller defense had limited Princeton to less than 70 yards of sustained offense. With nine minutes to go, the challenge was to prevent another big play, and stop a long, time-consuming drive as well. Princeton started with outstanding field position, eight yards away from the 50. Twice Mancuso gambled on fourth down and twice his team got the imperative yardage. The Moeller defense needed a break and got one on second down at the Moeller 27. On a quarterback option the pitchout missed its mark. Moeller recovered all the way back at the 41. Now it was up to the offense to play ball control. Brooks, who carried eight times in the tense touchdown march, ran it seven more times as the scoreboard clock kept blinking its way toward zero. Moeller ran nine plays in the last 3 minutes and 40 seconds. The last play carried to the Princeton 10.

Disappointed but not defeated, Princeton players promised to return with a vengeance a week later. "Look," said one to a sportswriter, "all we missed was an extra point. You watch. Next week we'll kick their tails all over the field. You write that down so everybody can see it."

11

The Recruiting Whirl

A friend speaking of Gerry once told this story:

A college coach called Moeller to discuss graduating senior football players.

"I've got two guys I'm sure can help your program," Gerry reportedly said.

"Great!" answered the college coach. "I'll be down in Cincinnati for next Friday's game."

Gerry provided the coach with a ticket, a parking pass, and a Moeller program, as was his custom. The coach arrived early to get a good seat. The score was close throughout the first half, and neither boy he had come to see was in on even one play. Moeller opened a more comfortable lead in the third period, but still the coach did not see his prospects in action. They did not play in the fourth quarter, either.

After the game, so the story goes, this disappointed, puzzled visitor rushed up to Gerry and said:

"Gerry! I thought you told me you had two players who could help me. I didn't see either one of them get in the game!"

"Coach," Gerry is said to have answered, "I said they could help *you,* not *me.*"

It may have been only a joke, but the point is well taken. More than 300 football players in Moeller's first 18 graduating classes—including a number of non-starters—received scholarships or other football-related financial aid in college. More than 70 of them played in the big time, for the likes of Ohio State, Michigan, Penn State, Florida State, Alabama, Louisiana State, North Carolina, Maryland, Colorado, Iowa State, Stanford, and, of course, Notre Dame. And Gerry placed another 50 or so at the other end of the college spectrum—at Georgetown, Adrian, Franklin, Ferris State, Benedictine, Wilmington, Hillsdale, Maryville, and Centre. He became an expert at both counseling the recruited and promoting the unrecruited.

At the end of each season Gerry would call his seniors together and ask, "How many of you want to go to college and play football? How many want to get aid?" In a typical group of 32 seniors, Gerry would usually count at least 25 hands. He would swallow hard and think to himself, "Wow! This is going to be a job!" Then he would knock himself out for four months to arrange an opportunity of some kind for at least an average of 20 of them each year.

Besides counting hands at his postseason senior meeting, Gerry taught a brief class in how to shake hands with a college coach, how to dress to impress a college coach, and how much to eat when dining with a college coach. College coaches are size-conscious, so Gerry told all of his seniors to wear a sweater over a shirt to every meeting with a recruiter or coach. "Sweaters make you look bulkier." If a boy lacked height, he was told to wear the biggest shoes he had, the ones with the highest heels. "Most of our kids who don't get big-time scholarships are passed over because of their lack of height." Gerry instructed his boys to politely decline second helpings when eating with a recruiter—even if they were hungry. "When they say, 'Here, have some more, have some more,' they're trying to find out whether this kid's the type who will take anything. They want unselfish kids, and this is a good test." And when it came to shaking hands, Gerry told them to grip firmly and look the coach straight in the eye. "A lot of kids are shy, especially around people they don't know. So, when a boy looks a coach in the eye and says, 'Nice to meet you, sir,' it leaves a lasting impression."

Being heavily recruited is both exciting and exhausting for a teen-age boy and his family. Few high school seniors, or their parents, are prepared for the chaos and pressure that comes with being courted by a succession of major college football recruiters whose jobs depend to a great extent on their ability to sell themselves and their school. Confronted with a mind-blowing, ego-inflating new experience, an athlete and his mom and dad generally

are ill-equipped for the agony of reaching a decision and the uncomfortable necessity of facing some likable men with the bad news
that their sales pitch failed.

Moeller stars have been the subjects of some fierce recruiting
jousts through the years. None, though, exceeded the lavish court-
ship of Steve Niehaus, the mammoth defensive tackle who signed
with Notre Dame in 1972, became an All-American, and was the
first player drafted by the Seattle Seahawks in their National Football League expansion year. Niehaus was a sophomore starter on
Moeller's unbeaten 1969 team when the first college recruiter
noticed him. Eighteen seniors played college football from that team
and nine junior teammates followed a year later, but "The Rookie,"
as his coaches called him then, still stood out in the talented crowd.

"Notre Dame came down to look at our films and check out a
couple of guys," Gerry said. "They got the numbers mixed up and
thought Steve was a senior. They went back and a few days later
called us to find out for sure who he was. They were going to offer
him a scholarship right away—until they found out he was a
sophomore!" Ultimately, 150 schools approached Niehaus. "He
was the first kid we had who could have gone any place he
wanted," Gerry said. "Usually a school calls Moeller and begins by
asking, 'Who do you have?' That year it started with, 'Is Steve
Niehaus interested in us?' "

Gerry shielded his players from the distractions of college recruitment during the season. College coaches were welcome to
attend practice from August through November. "This allows them
to get a good line on the kids, ability-wise and size-wise," Gerry
said. They were invited to attend as many games as they could;
Gerry would provide a ticket and a good seat. "We encourage them
to come to the games," he said, "because then they get to see the
boy in action." But they could not come to the school to watch films
during the season, because the Moeller coaches and players needed
access to the films at all times. All mail sent by colleges to Moeller
players was stored in large boxes until the season ended, when
student managers would sort and deliver four month's worth to the
seniors at once. Telephone calls from college coaches, alumni, or
students to any Moeller football player also were verboten throughout the season.

"When a kid's a senior, we want him thinking one thing, and
that's Moeller football," Gerry said. "We don't want him thinking
other things. I know it hurt me a little bit when I was playing high

school football and scouts talked to me before a game. I pressed a little harder because I knew they were there; I didn't play well."

Gerry's players alerted him anytime anyone associated with a college athletic program attempted to speak to them. Even the parents would report transgressions. He once called a Big Ten school and told the coach, who was a friend of his, "If this continues, you can just forget about getting transcripts out of here." In this case the telephone calls, from an overzealous assistant coach, ceased immediately.

If parents could be as independent and self-assured as Gerry, it would make the adventure of recruitment so much easier and more enjoyable. Most of them, though, try to be cooperative and patient with recruiters because they fear jeopardizing their son's chances of a scholarship at the school he wants to attend. Recruiters are trying to win the parents' friendship and trust, so parents usually worry about being rude or hurting a man's feelings if they do not receive him cordially at all times. It is flattering to have 20 or 30 coaches tell them their son is a great athlete, so they are reluctant to reduce the field of contenders too early in the game. "Kids and parents are on an ego trip during this time," Gerry said, "which is quite natural."

Most parents do not realize until it is too late that they can control the disruption in their home, and reduce stress and strain on them and their son during his final deliberations, by simply laying down some ground rules and firmly but politely insisting that all recruiters observe them. It still is not easy. Recruiters are salesmen, persistent salesmen. The best ones are not easily discouraged. The parents and their son must have enough self-discipline to enforce their rules and not begin granting exceptions. During intensive recruiting, an exception granted one recruiter quickly becomes the rule applied, in fairness, to all.

"The best advice I can give to parents," Gerry said, "is to analyze every coach and every school the first time they come into the home. Is your boy going to be treated the same way after recruitment and signing as he was during the recruiting period? Most people can judge sincerity. If they reduce the number of schools they are going to seriously consider as early as possible, it will make an unbelieveable difference later on.

"The second thing is, I would advise they set a certain limit on phone calls. A lot of our kids' parents told recruiters they could call once a week. Set a time and a night, and tell them: 'This is your night and your time. I don't want any calls from alumni; I don't want any calls from anybody else. This is your time, your night, and I'll be there. You won't be frustrated.' If they do that and the coaches don't abide by it, then they should nix that school. If they watch how a coach abides by it, it will help them make a decision about the coach as a person and the school as one that follows rules."

Recruiting season begins with a flurry of home visits by the recruiters. A so-called blue-chipper may have 30 or 40 coaches ask permission to stop by to introduce themselves, meet the boy and his parents, and invite the boy to make a campus visit. "A heavily recruited athlete should not commit to visit anywhere unless he's *sure* that's one of the schools he definitely may want to attend," Gerry said. "He'll be bombarded the first three weeks."

Choosing which schools to visit is the first tough decision an athlete will face. The National Collegiate Athletic Association allows six visits at the expense of the host schools. If an athlete wants to visit more than six universities, he can go only if he pays his own way to the others.

"The boy should make a list of the weekends that he wants to make visits," Gerry said. "He should get that squared away before the college coaches start coming in. He should check with the coach of the sport he is playing at that time, if he's playing another sport, to be sure he schedules visits around the team's schedule. And there are bound to be a couple of schools each athlete will definitely want to visit, even before the coach calls. A boy should save visits for those schools and find out their best weekends for visits before committing to others. After he has seen those two, he should sit down and sort out the rest with his parents.

"It's best to pick a certain date, a few weeks after recruiting season starts, and tell the coaches, when they visit the first time, to check back then, by telephone, to see if the boy wants to make a visit to their school. The boy should be prepared to say definitely, yes or no, at that time. It's much easier to tell a person no on the phone than it is in person."

Gerry recalled one outstanding Moeller player who could not say no to any coach. He accepted six visits, made them all, and then came to Gerry in tears because he had three more schools he wanted to check out. Gerry offered his car to the boy but told him he would have to pay for his own gas and expenses. They talked for a long time and the boy finally decided there was no need to visit more schools after all. He chose to attend one of his original six. Until the National Collegiate Athletic Association adopted the six-visit rule, high school athletes were permitted to visit as many campuses as they wanted at the expense of the colleges; but Gerry always limited his seniors to five trips.

"I figured a kid could make up his mind in five visits," he said. "If he was gone more than five weekends, it was going to hurt his grades, and he was going to get tired of it, and he was going to get confused." Even after he relaxed his rule to agree with the NCAA, Gerry still advised his players to schedule only five visits. "Keep one open for a late-comer," he said.

A campus visit is two or three days of VIP treatment, parties, good food, and pretty coeds. It is great fun. It is also very serious business; the recruit is exploring the place that may become his home for much of the next four years of his life. The hospitality sometimes can obstruct the perception of an impressionable young man. "A kid should have a lot of questions in his mind that he expects to be answered during the visit," Gerry said. "He should check out everything he'll be using at the school."

The most important part of the visit, in Gerry's opinion, is the hour or two the boy will spend meeting one-on-one with the head coach.

"The boy has to make sure the head coach is honest with him," Gerry said. "It is very important that the boy knows what the coach's plans are for him. If he's a quarterback, or if he's a running back or a wide receiver, what kind of offense is the coach going to run? If he's a receiver, it is a waste of time for him to go to a triple option school; he should go to a school where they throw the ball. If he's a drop-back quarterback and he can go to an option school, it is very important to know if they are going to change their offense for him since they're recruiting him that heavily.

"A boy has to know how many people are ahead of him, and what the coach thinks of those people. Also, what other players is the school recruiting at the boy's position? Does the coach think another prospect has more potential, if he can get him? These are things a boy should ask; most of them will not, though. But a head coach who is an honest head coach should convey this to the boy so the athlete knows where he stands. Then, if he chooses the university, he is less likely to be disappointed.

"The boy should see how he hits it off with the head coach. That's very important. Is the head coach interested in him as a person? Or is he just interested in him as a number? Is the head coach the kind of person who is going to help him out when he has problems? Who is the assistant coach for the position he's going to play? How will the coach who recruits him take care of him while he's in school? Will he look after him as a second father? How does the head coach relate to his assistants?"

During a visit it also is important to meet professors and discuss courses of study; to attend a sporting event and observe the spirit of the student body and alumni; to talk to the athletes themselves and find out how they feel about their coaches and the athletic program; and to sample the social life, because it is an important part of college. "He's going to go there for an education," Gerry said, "and an education is a varied thing. Sports add to an education; the social life adds to an education. It's all part of growing up."

Since recruiting rules limit a player's campus visits and his face-to-face contact with each recruiter, major colleges enlist the aid of alumni to supplement the coach's appearances. The president of Continental Airlines, all-pro defensive tackle Mike Reid, and a wealthy industrialist who later became United States ambassador to Switzerland were among the luminaries who contacted Steve Niehaus on behalf of the universities competing for his talents. Other supporters kept him busy three or four nights a week, usually taking him to dinner. It reached the point where a dinner invitation was an instant turnoff. Niehaus estimated he ate 45 pounds of steak during the recruiting season. According to his bathroom scale he gained 20 pounds.

For the record, Niehaus said he was not offered anything illegal by any coach or alumnus. Gerry knows of only one attempt to influence a Moeller player's decision. Jay Case, like Niehaus a prep All-American at defensive tackle, was making one of his campus visits in 1974 when a booster approached him at a party, shoved a large sum of money into his pocket and said, "Here's some spending money for the weekend. You can work for me this summer." Case met with the school's head coach the next day and returned the money. The coach was embarrassed; he told Case he had not known that sort of thing was happening at his school. Gerry realizes it is almost impossible to prove that a coach has knowledge of such acts by alumni or that he approves of them. But, he says, "If they know the head coach is aware of it and condoning it, he should be barred from college coaching." Case became another Moeller export to Notre Dame, his decision influenced greatly by the attempt to buy him for another school.

When the week of decision arrived for Steve Niehaus, representatives from the schools that still had a chance practically stood in line at the Niehaus front door. Alabama came to call on Monday night; Colorado had from 6 to 8 o'clock on Tuesday evening and Notre Dame 8 to 10:30. The folks from Colorado and the folks from Notre Dame missed passing each other on the sidewalk by minutes. Wednesday night belonged to Michigan, and Thursday night was reserved for Woody Hayes himself. The telephone kept ringing as recruiters and alumni called "just to keep in touch, just to keep you thinking about us and to let you know we're thinking about you." Steve finally asked his dad for the car keys and finished sorting out his thoughts while he went for a drive, alone.

It is common for conference-member schools to sign or attempt to sign prospects to conference letters of intent. These bind the player to the signing school within its conference but are not binding outside that conference. Thus, an athlete could sign a dozen conference letters of intent. Gerry discouraged his players from doing so. "Some kids would sign a letter of intent for a different conference each week," he said. "That just puts more pressure on them when they finally have to sign the national letter of intent with one school. I feel you should make a commitment to only one school, and you should honor that commitment."

Gerry advised his players to reach their decision before the national signing day. "A boy should make it the night before and avoid the tremendous pressure that comes with keeping recruiters on the line until the last possible second," he said. "He should call the other coaches ahead of time and tell them of his decision. They're going to try to sell him on still going to their school. This is the time he's got to get up and say, 'Coach, I've made my decision. I appreciate it, but this is where I'm going to school, and I don't want to talk to you any more about it. I really want to thank you for being fair with me, being good with me and being my friend.' And if the coach continues, the boy should tell him, 'Coach, I'm going to hang up because I've made my decision. Now, I want to thank you.' "

Most major colleges will actively recruit roughly twice as many athletes as they have scholarships to award. This is their way of hedging their bets. But most athletes and parents forget that there are three other recruits at the same position, in line for the same scholarship at the same school if they turn it down for another offer. It may not seem so at the moment, even as the recruiter urges them to reconsider and refuses to accept no for a final answer, but they actually are doing him a favor by informing him as soon as they reach a decision.

"It's important to tell a coach as soon as they've eliminated him," Gerry said, "because it gives him an opportunity to go after someone else. There are so many good athletes in the country! There are only about five or ten who are really going to make a difference in a program by themselves. Coaches talk about the top twenty-five in the country—I want to tell you, besides those top twenty-five, there's another two thousand who are just as good. Parents don't realize that."

Maybe half of the Moeller seniors who continued into college football each year were virtually assured of something good going into recruiting season. But the rest relied heavily on Gerry's salesmanship and benefitted greatly from his credibility as a talent scout for all levels of college football. In 1977, for example, a husky, hard-working offensive lineman named Kevin Greve had potential but had not been able to crack the Moeller starting lineup. Gerry landed him a full ride at Eastern Kentucky University. Greve continued to work diligently in the weight room and by his junior year was considered Eastern's most valuable lineman and a pro prospect.

Gerry would prepare a promotional packet on each player he was trying to place. The envelope contained a letter from Gerry with a confidential evaluation of the boy as a football player and a person, a Moeller program, a game film showing the boy at his best, his scholastic transcript and an information sheet listing name, address, home phone, height, weight, speed in the 40-yard dash, jersey number, test scores, and class rank. He would call coaches and write letters until he had arranged a visit somewhere. Then he would give the boy his dossier and send him off. Whenever possible, Gerry would set up a visit to the same school for three or four players at the same time so they could share the cost. Usually, if Gerry got a player as far as an interview with a coach, the boy would be offered something.

"If I recommended a kid, the college coach knew I wasn't going to exaggerate or lie to him. After they get to know you, if they know you're going to have two or three kids a year and they know you're always square with them, they'll listen to you. It's impossible for them to cover any city or any state and know every great athlete. And there's always a sleeper. The key is for the high school coach to know what level his kids can play; you're so high on your own kids that you don't think there's anybody who has a better player. And then you have to be honest with the boy and tell him where you think he can play. That's hard because the reason they're great high school players is because they have complete belief in themselves. Now you've got to sit down and temper that belief a little bit."

Gerry knew how to get the most out of college programs that awarded aid solely on the basis of financial need—Ivy League, NCAA Division III, and NAIA (National Association of Intercollegiate Athletics) schools. He also was adept at cleaning up the leftovers at the end of the recruiting season. "March or late February is the time when you can pick up things for kids," he said. "All the schools are shooting for the same kids, and only so many can be taken at a certain school. There are scholarships left because they didn't get all the kids they were going after."

Not every player Gerry placed in college played four more years of football. "When our kids go to a small school it's a tough adjustment the first six months," he admitted, "because they play in front of smaller crowds, the equipment isn't as good, and they don't have as big a coaching staff. It's a very difficult change for a kid to go from the top high school in the country to one of the smaller college programs in the country. It's a big adjustment after he's been playing in the limelight and been in a program like ours."

THE END OF AN ERA

PLAYOFF ROUND ONE: MOELLER vs. PRINCETON

November 7, 1980

* * *

PLAYOFF ROUND TWO: MOELLER vs. UPPER ARLINGTON

November 14, 1980

The gymnasium was dark. Dan Ledford stood in the audio-visual room high above the gym floor, a reel-to-reel tape recorder at his side. Two slide projectors were aimed through an open window toward a huge screen suspended in front of the stage at the other end of the basketball floor. The tape started rolling and the prodigious introduction to the theme from *Superman* heralded that the Moeller state playoffs pep rally, the biggest and best of the year, had begun. With Dan's narration blended over the music, slides of magazine layouts and newspaper clippings were testimony to the football team's wide acclaim.

The grand orchestral strains faded and were replaced by the fast beat of electric guitars, drums, and the magical synthesizer. It was the Academy Award-winning title song from the movie *FAME* — a perfect choice. The adrenalin began to flow as actress Irene Cara sang:

"Baby, look at me
"And tell me what you see
"You ain't seen the best of me yet
"Give me time, I'll make you forget the rest . . ."

Dan was working both projectors with one hand-held control, moving his arm to the music, activating one projector, then the other, back and forth. One image no sooner dissolved than another took its place. All the time, Irene Cara was singing:

"I can catch the moon in my hand
"Don't you know who I am? Remember my name!"

The faces of the Moeller seniors and coaches, and glimpses of them in action appeared, as if from within the screen, then disappeared just as mysteriously. Jeff Lytton, the center . . . a power sweep . . . tackle Doug Williams . . . the offensive line pass blocking . . . Steve Klonne . . . players prostrate in the Nippert Stadium end zone, stretching their legs before a game . . . Tony Melink kicking off . . . a crushing tackle . . . . And all the time, Irene Cara was singing:

"FAME!

"I'm going to make it to heaven

"Light up the sky like a flame

"FAME!

"I'm going to live forever

"Baby, remember my name . . . Remember, Remember, Remember . . ."

The music died away and the voice of Bill Sorrell, play-by-play announcer on Moeller's radio broadcasts, filled the void as the smiling face of Mark Brooks was projected onto the screen, followed closely by slides of him in action.

"Moeller has the ball on the St. Xavier twenty-three. It's second down and Tim Jolley is in at quarterback. He hands to Mark Brooks, off left tackle. Mark bounces outside, then cuts behind a block . . . he's in the clear! He might go all the way . . . he's going to . . . He does! Mark Brooks, seventy-seven yards and Moeller can tie this game up with the extra point . . ."

The cheering of the crowd reached its peak in the background and Irene Cara returned, singing:

"FAME!

"I feel it coming together . . ."

The soft, soothing sound of a single piano, "Dressing Room Piano" from *Fame,* accompanied a slide that read, simply: GERRY FAUST. Over tranquil notes played like syllables spoken to a lip-reader, Dan Ledford's voice was heard:

"Gerry Faust . . . None of us here at Moeller know, Gerry, if this will be our last season with you or not . . . But in case it is, we want to say . . . Thanks . . ."

Dozens of slides followed; Gerry shouting, Gerry pointing, Gerry laughing, Gerry praying . . . hugging his players and chewing them out. It was a moving tribute. It ended with the unmistakable, contagious beat of the rock group Queen. "Another One Bites the Dust" ushered in a series of word slides that read, in succession: MOELLER, PRIDE, GCL, CITY, STATE, and, finally, PRINCETON, Tonight.

"I hope the players aren't as tired as the coaches are," Ted Bacigalupo said wearily in midweek. Even unsinkable Gerry was showing the strain of preparing two weeks in a row for a team as dangerous as Princeton. During the only quiet moment he had experienced in weeks, Gerry slumped into a chair in the coaches' office and said to Terry Lichtenberg, his newest addition to the staff: "Lichty, I'm so tired. The pressure's unbelievable." Lichtenberg, whose brother, Tom, joined Gerry's first staff at Notre Dame, thought he might actually have a chance to talk alone with Gerry for a few minutes, but the best opportunity of the season ended abruptly with (what else?) a phone call. Jim Higgins finally just slept until noon one school day. "This is the toughest year by far," he said. "The toughest schedule, Princeton back-to-back, an extra week of playoffs, and the Notre Dame thing hanging over us all year. There just hasn't been a break."

Gerry went through with his promise to dress all 76 members of the varsity and seat 16 of them in the stands in order to comply with the state playoffs edict that no team have more than 60 players on the field. To the boys who would be sitting among the spectators, he said: "Do the best job you can—stay together and pray." To the lucky 60 he said: "Those kids worked their butts off this week. They made you a better football team. You can go out and get this one for them."

The close score of the regular-season game the week before and expectations of a repeat performance brought more people to Nippert Stadium than any football game since the Bengals moved their games from Nippert to Riverfront Stadium in 1970. Fans stood on the roofs of buildings surrounding the stadium, climbed poles, and lined up 10 deep behind a chain link fence that ran along one side of the stadium. The total turnout easily was 30,000 people. The night had all the color and excitement of a college bowl game, but the rematch turned out to be a mismatch.

Moeller unloaded weapons Princeton had not encountered in the first game, and those broke the game wide open. Quarterback Mike Willging, who attempted only five short passes in Game One, fired touchdown bombs of 31 and 48 yards on Moellers' second and third possessions of Game Two. The receivers were wide open both times; plays run in the first game had set them up. Sophomore Hiawatha Francisco, who lived up to his immense potential for the first time all season, added a decisive dimension to the Moeller ground game. Hiawatha, or Hi, or "H," or Francisco, as Gerry variously called him through the season, ran the ball 23 times and gained 121 yards while Princeton was laying for Mark Brooks. He also caught the 48-yard touchdown pass. Brooks, despite Princeton's efforts to slow him down, added 90 yards on 24 carries and scored twice. His second touchdown, an unnecessary one with seven seconds left in the game, made the final score 28–3.

"Why are those kids sitting in the stands?" The question opened Gerry's postgame press conference. He explained, then begged all sportswriters to lay off the story. "If you write anything about it now," he said, "it's liable to make the commissioner mad, and then he'll just say we can't even do that. It would only hurt the kids. I agree it's a dumb rule, and I'd like to see something written about it. But please, wait until after the playoffs." It would not be nearly as good a story after the playoffs, the writers sighed, yet they granted Gerry his wish. The reporters changed the subject, but he did not want to talk about Notre Dame, either.

"Let's talk about this game we just played," Gerry said. "All I'm interested in right now is helping this team win two more games."

Anyone who was looking closely for indications about the direction of Gerry's career would have found one during the week of the second playoff game with Upper Arlington. Gerry conducted one of his eighth grade orientation sessions, and Dan Ledford sat in the back of the room, learning the routine. It had been decided that Dan would inherit that part of Gerry's job, if Gerry did leave. Pressed for time, Gerry advanced the slides so rapidly they were almost superimposed over one another on the screen. His talk was one, long, run-on sentence with a comma after every fourth slide to allow a deep breath.

"I want to talk to you about the value of a Catholic education," he began. "The most important thing is to get a Catholic education. Why? To be a better person . . ." A collage of magazine and newspaper clippings flashed across the screen. "Every paper you pick up, every newspaper, it's Moeller, Moeller, Moeller! It's the greatest high school in the country . . ." He came to a slide of the chapel. "Students can go to Mass every morning at seven forty-five; I think it's a great way to start the day . . ." The Moeller faculty and staff, a typical day at school, and examples of course offerings all passed quickly before the eighth graders' eyes; then clubs, activities, and athletics. "We're number one in football; I think you know that.

You don't have to be big to play football here; we have Tim King, who's only five-nine and one-sixty. This is a chance to play for the best football team in the nation . . ." When he came to a slide of one student helping another, Gerry said: "You know, there's more to life than football, basketball, and studies. There are the finer things, like art and music, and there's helping people. Each Christmas the Moeller boys go to Children's Hospital, and some of them are Big Brothers. And what is that? That's Christianity, and that's what we teach here at Moeller High School." The next slide showed a Marianist brother. "After four years, we hope some of you will have a vocation and become a priest or a religious." The last slide in the carousel was a shot of Moeller High. "Why is Moeller the best? One word: Spirit! You're going to be the Class of '85. With your spirit, just imagine what Moeller High School can be!"

After the presentation, Dan Ledford frowned as he helped pack up. "Gerry," he joked, "I think you should speed up your delivery a little."

A note from Father Rudemiller, Gerry's old adversary at Elder, arrived early in the week. Father Rudy had been named pastor at a church only minutes from Welcome Stadium in Dayton where Moeller's second-round playoff game against Upper Arlington would be played. Since he was so near, he decided to attend. Gerry addressed an envelope to Rudy as soon as he read the note. He mailed it promptly, too. Only thing was, he forgot to put a ticket in it. When Rudy opened the empty envelope, he smiled and decided not to mention it to Gerry, who obviously had a lot on his mind.

On game night Moeller arrived at Welcome Stadium, coincidentally, just as Rudy walked toward a ticket booth.

"Father Rudy! Didn't you get the ticket?" Gerry could not understand why Rudy was *paying* his way into the game.

Rudy explained and Gerry was distraught. "Don't buy a ticket! I'll get you in!"

Gerry dug into his pockets and came up empty. He was out of tickets. He looked around, spotting one of the team doctors.

"Let me have your pass; I'll get you in."

Rudy protested; Gerry handed him the pass, then reconsidered. "Here! Here's five dollars!"

Rudy objected again. "I can pay my own way in," he said. "It's no big deal."

Gerry was frantic; he had let a friend down. The game did not seem to matter at that moment. He led Rudy to the gate.

"He's with me," Gerry said. The man at the gate did not have a chance.

Typical Gerry, Father Rudy smiled to himself.

Questions about the players in the stands came up again after Moeller outclassed Upper Arlington, a suburban Columbus school that was a three-time wire service poll state champion in the late 1960s. Reserve tailback Lindsey Montgomery, the biggest spirit man in uniform, realized the rare thrill of scoring a state playoffs touchdown—albeit with nine seconds left in the game—to complete a 36–0 romp. The subs and starters had resembled hockey players as they climbed over the wall in front of the first row of seats, exchanging places with 4:53 left in the game.

Some of the players who spent the Princeton game in the stands had gone to their assistant coaches during the following week of practice, asking to be spared the embarrassment of being so clearly designated a substitute. Football players in helmets and shoulder pads do look a little out of place among people in hats and coats. But Gerry dismissed their objections; they were part of the team and they belonged in uniform. Dayton and Columbus writers inquired about it, but they, too, gave in to Gerry's pleas not to "spoil it" for those boys.

The next night the other giant in Ohio high school football—famous Massillon—earned its ticket to the finals by knocking off an unbeaten Cleveland-area team, Willoughby South. The state championship game was going to provide a storybook ending to Gerry's last season at Moeller.

"For the first time," observed Jeff Leibert, "we'll be up against a team with the kind of tradition and intensity we have at Moeller. Massillon won't be awed playing Moeller."

12

The Men of Moeller

The lettering on the locker room door reads, "Through These Doors Walk the Men of Moeller." There is a tendency, at first, to think only of greatness: 22 high school All-Americans . . . 34 all-staters . . . Steve Sylvester of Oakland's two-time Super Bowl champion Raiders, voted the NFL's most versatile lineman in 1979 . . . Steve Niehaus . . . . But Moeller football under Gerry was more than superstars and All-Americans. It was more than undefeated seasons and state or national championships. It was a community, where teen-age boys were taught discipline and responsibility, where total dedication was demanded, and effort rewarded with respect and consideration, if not always personal stardom.

The Men of Moeller included George the organist, Jack the manager-trainer, Wayne the courageous, Greg the determined, Tugboat the stubborn, Rick the faithful, and hundreds of others, many of whom did not play, did not start, or did not star. The Men of Moeller in some cases were blessed with special athletic talents and had to learn to live with their fame at a young age, had to learn self-control, and had to learn humility. But mostly they were average kids. The Men of Moeller worked hard, loved each other, and discovered that disappointment could have a reason and things really do work out for the best if you help them along.

Stardom seemed a certainty for Eric Ellington the first time he walked through those doors to the Moeller locker room. He was faster than any back in Moeller history, and he could bob and weave and cut without slowing up. As a freshman, he played on the sophomore team. As a sophomore, he was the varsity's leading rusher. By the start of his senior season, he had already gained 1,070 yards, more than any underclassman before him. He was great. But Gerry was not satisfied with Eric Ellington. "Eric, as a junior, would be late to practice once in awhile—not too often, but we'd have to get on him once in awhile. And he'd go out on the field, and when he wasn't feeling well, he wouldn't put out. It was my fault, because I'd babied him for two or three years."

Ellington was in line to be a Moeller captain his senior year. The team elected four captains, but the vote was not binding. The coaches used the team's preferences as a guide, but considered other factors, too. The final choice was theirs—Gerry's actually. And, though Eric Ellington had finished second in the voting, he was not going to be one of Moeller's 1979 captains. "I called Eric and his mother, and we met in the cafeteria. I told him he was always saying things we wanted to hear; and he had not really worked at it or set an example. I told him I knew he wanted to be captain, and he was chosen by his teammates. But, I wasn't going to let him be captain, because I didn't think he deserved to be captain because of the way he went at football and things like that."

When Gerry said, "Eric, you've been a con artist for the last two or three years here," Eric's mother pounded her fist on the cafeteria table.

"Eric," she said, "you've been the same way at home. You've been a con artist for the last couple of years, and when I tell you to do something, you don't do it; you talk your way out of it."

Gerry remembers seeing tears come to Eric Ellington's eyes. "I think he finally realized that the two people who cared for him probably more than anybody were trying to tell him something. They were trying to tell him that he had a lot of potential as a person, but he lacked some of the qualities that were necessary to be that person."

Gerry then put things in perspective. "You have two ways to go," he told Eric. "You can sulk about it, and it will just prove my point that you don't deserve to be captain; or you can go and really attack things, really change your approach and prove that I was wrong."

Eric Ellington ran for 1,013 yards his senior year, third best single-season total in school history. He scored 96 points, second best single-season total in school history. Against Brother Rice High School of Detroit, he gained 178 yards in only 10 carries. He was named Ohio's Player of the Year and ended his career as Moeller's all-time leading ground-gainer with 2,083 yards. "He had a phenomenal year," Gerry says proudly. "He never missed practice—was never even a minute late. He was a leader. He worked." Eric Ellington virtually had his choice of college scholarships and chose Louisiana State—two years later the opposing team in Gerry's debut as Notre Dame's head coach!

* * *

Jack Muenchen was not very big, and he lacked Eric Ellington's speed. "Of all the kids we've had," Gerry said, "he'd have to rank up there as one of the kids with the most heart." But, 120-pound centers just do not play football at Moeller High School. Gerry kept Jack Muenchen in the football program through his junior year, but when his senior season approached, Gerry knew he would have to make a very difficult decision. Gerry and Jack Muenchen's dad are close friends, and Mr. Muenchen had contributed to the Moeller football program in many ways during its formative years.

"But it had reached the point that Jack was losing some friends because they felt he was on the team only because his dad and I were so close," Gerry said. "So, for his own good, I cut the kid, because I didn't want him to lose his relationship with his peers. Well, it really broke the kid's heart. I mean it really broke the kid's heart. So I called his father and told him what I had done, and his dad was really upset. I mean really upset! His dad really wanted Jack to be a football player, and Jack wanted to be a football player. It really bothered me because his dad was a very good friend of mine and had done a lot for Moeller."

Gerry spent two hours on the telephone with Mr. Muenchen. "I tried to tell him that God didn't bless this kid with the ability to be a football player and it was causing problems; that he was losing his friends."

A day later, Gerry asked Jack Muenchen to be a student trainer/manager; he accepted immediately even though his father, still hurt, found it all so hard to accept. "Munch was probably one of the best we've ever had. He was a trainer and manager the way he was a football player, and as the season went on, Munch was so respected by his peers because he did everything." Jack Muenchen received a college scholarship as a manager/trainer, landed a summer job as trainer for the Cincinnati Reds' Tampa, Florida, farm team, then became a high school athletic trainer and opened a medical equipment business in Florida.

"Jack's dad and I have talked about how God works in strange ways," Gerry says. "It was a thing that was very touchy and very difficult at first, but it ended up being what God really wanted for him in the long run."

* * *

George Becker had no desire to be a football player, and during his first few days as a Moeller freshman, he experienced the loneliness that comes with being new. Then a couple of football players took time to notice, stop, and reach out to him. They talked to George Becker and learned that he did not know anyone in the school and he felt alone. They also learned that he played the organ. The football players went to Gerry and asked if George, their new friend, could play the organ during the team's chapel services. Of course he could.

"When the kid came up for the first time," Gerry recalls, "he was scared to death. Every other note was off-key. But afterwards all the kids went up and shook his hand and thanked him for being part of the team. The next week he was great."

George the organist earned a letter-sweater and traveled with the team for four years. It is one of Gerry's favorite stories. "The kids took time out to find out what was wrong with another human being. You try to put that across to kids, and when you see it done without you promoting it, when they do it on their own, it really makes you feel good."

* * *

The charges of illegal recruiting began the day Jim Brown—six feet six and 250 pounds, black and non-Catholic—walked into Moeller High School. But he was there, instead of the nearby public school, for a very personal reason. His father, a widower, wanted the boy in the kind of disciplined, structured environment that Moeller provides. He wanted him kept busy after school, and he hoped his son's unusual size might be applied in a way that might benefit him in life. Mr. Brown wanted his mammoth son to become a football player. His father paid Jim's tuition the first year, but it was understood that as soon as Jim reached the age of 16, he would need to get a job and pay the rest himself. It was during that freshman year that Gerry grew to love Jim Brown. Working out in the weight room one day, Jim found a watch that someone had left behind. Without a car of his own, he made his way to Gerry's home two miles away.

"Coach, I locked up the weight room, and I found this watch," he said to Gerry.

"Jim, do you have a watch?"

"No, sir; I've never owned a watch."

Jim Brown's honesty made Gerry feel good inside. Later, when the team presented Gerry with a new watch, he gave his old one to Jim Brown.

When the future All-American turned 16, Gerry helped him get a job and made sure his earnings were not misspent. "Jimmy had to bring his paycheck to me every week. I'd take it to school and cash it and give him five dollars spending money." Once that first year Jim Brown asked for more than five dollars. A wedding was coming up and he wanted to get a new suit. "Jimmy," Gerry said, "I can't do it. You've got to get your tuition paid." It seemed cold-hearted to Gerry's wife. "How can you do that to him?" Marlene objected. Her husband would not waver. "He's got to get his tuition paid. If someone doesn't help him save it, he'll never save it on his own." Jim Brown kept it up for three years, became a high school All-American, and was a starting offensive tackle at Penn State by his sophomore season. He appeared headed for a spectacular college career until he suffered a broken ankle the following spring.

* * *

In a sport where only the strong survive, Wayne Morrison did not figure to have much of a future in Moeller football. An illness at birth had left him with some slight paralysis in one arm and shoulder. His parents were concerned that their son might develop a passive attitude, a give-up attitude, because of his limitation. Mr. Morrison spoke to Gerry, and Gerry spoke to the boy.

"Son," he said, "you'll never be able to block or tackle, but God gave you two strong legs. If you're willing to work hard enough, you can become the placekicker for this team."

The progress was slow, but Wayne Morrison persevered. "Between his junior and senior years he improved so much it was unbelievable," Gerry recalls. In his senior year, Wayne Morrison converted 37 of 41 extra point attempts and made three field goals in eight tries, including one from 47 yards. His single-season total of 46 points ranked third among Moeller kickers. He earned a scholarship to the University of Virginia where, as a freshman, he made 20 of 32 extra points and 9 of 16 field goal attempts, including a 50-yarder against Navy. In his sophomore season, he won three games with field goals.

* * *

Wayne Morrison got his chance because Gerry was careful about which players he cut and which ones he kept. "You've got room on a football team to keep kids for different reasons," he believes. "I've kept kids on the team who have had a tough home life and it was important for them to be in a family-type atmosphere. I've kept kids who didn't ever succeed at anything in life and just making the team would be a success for them. You always have room for one or two kids."

Gerry cannot remember Tugboat's real name to this day, "because I called him 'Tugboat' for so long." Tugboat stood five feet six inches tall and weighed about 210—strong but small, like a tugboat. Gerry told him his junior year: "We'll carry you this year, but we can't carry you next year. We just can't carry that many seniors." But, when the winter quickness drills began after Tugboat's junior season had ended, he was there. And, he was in the weight room as regularly as anyone else. And when summer practice finally rolled around, Tugboat asked if he could try out. "Yes, you can come out," Gerry relented, "but your chances of making it are almost nil." As expected, Gerry cut Tugboat. "We just can't keep you, Tugboat. I told you last year." And Tugboat said, "I want to thank you, Mr. Faust."

When practice was about to start that day, Gerry made his customary sweep through the locker room, to chase out the stragglers. There on a bench by the door lay Tugboat, face down. "Tugboat, go turn in your uniform," he said. But Tugboat would not move. A telephone call provided a momentary interruption, but when Gerry returned, Tugboat still had not budged. "Tugboat, turn in your uniform," he repeated. The boy would not move, would not speak. Gerry was touched. "All right! Go out and start practicing; you'll be on the team." Tugboat jumped to his feet and beat his soft-hearted coach out the door. Tugboat did not mind that he rarely played in varsity games his senior season. He was on the team. And he made a contribution. "He was one of the most valuable members of our team," Gerry said. "The kids loved him; he was always lifting everybody's spirits. And in practice he gave us everything he had. He helped us have a great ball club."

"Vida Blue's" real name is Rick Keller, and, unlike Tugboat, he was an athlete. "But he was in a position where we had a lot of really good athletes, and he wasn't the size to be able to play another position," Gerry said. The coaches decided to cut him as a senior. Gerry called Vida Blue into his office and explained why he was being cut; Gerry always met individually with the players who did not make the team. "I don't have much respect for any coach who puts up a list of guys who made it or guys who didn't, and doesn't sit down and talk with each kid who gets cut. Because that kid put a lot of time in, and I feel you owe him an explanation."

Rick Keller said he understood, thanked Gerry for the three years, and said he really enjoyed it and really got a lot out of being on the team.

It was the last day of cuts, and those players who would comprise the varsity team that year were about to meet with Gerry. "There are a lot of guys who want to be on the squad," he would tell them, "and you've been privileged to be included on the ball club, so we expect certain things from you." On his way to that meeting, Gerry took a shortcut through the chapel. He glanced at the altar.

"I look, and there's Vida Blue! In there praying! I said to myself, 'There's no way I'm going to cut a kid who, after he gets cut, is in the chapel praying!' A guy's got a commitment to God if after one of the biggest disappointments in his life he's up there praying. That's quality."

Gerry told him: "Get your uniform." Rick Keller was popular with his teammates, and his return meant a lot to them. It turned out, too, that Rick Keller was needed in the lineup as Moeller went undefeated and won state and national championships. He returned three years later, while still in college, to help coach the Moeller freshmen.

* * *

There were, of course, many boys cut from the Moeller football team each year who could have played, perhaps even started, at other high schools. And there were many boys who enrolled at

Moeller admittedly to fulfill a dream of playing for the best high school football team in the nation. Greg Schube was one. He came 20 miles from a northern suburb every day, a non-Catholic who attended Moeller High School because he wanted to be a Moeller football player. Gerry cut him as a junior and encouraged him to transfer to his neighborhood public school, where he might have been a starter.

"I went home pretty disappointed," Schube says. "My dad said he still loved me; he told me I didn't have to play football for him. He said I could transfer if I wanted to." But Greg Schube stayed at Moeller. And every day for the first seven weeks of that season, he attended practice on his own, running laps and watching, studying. "I figured if I was around, I'd pick up some things for next year."

Impressed by such persistence, Gerry gave the young man a uniform the eighth week and told him he was back on the team. It was a decision that upset the whole coaching staff. "Every kid you cut will think he can get back on the team," his assistants predicted. "Yeah, but every kid I cut hasn't been up on that practice field for the last seven weeks," Gerry answered. Greg Schube grew a lot during the next summer, returned as a mature senior, and played often as a defensive back on another of Moeller's unbeaten state and national champs.

"God may not bless some kids athletically," Gerry says of the Rick Kellers and Greg Schubes, "but he blesses them with intensity and with the desire to succeed or the desire to be something to such a degree that they make up for the lack of ability in other ways. Sure, we had a lot of kids come to Moeller to play football who couldn't make it. But we lost very few of those kids from the school. They may have come to Moeller at first for football, but after they were here they found out that the school is a great school academically, discipline-wise and spirit-wise. They come to love the school and they get themselves involved in other things and really become outstanding in other areas."

* * *

Gerry never told the Men of Moeller not to smoke or drink; he did not discuss drugs. "We never bring up those subjects because our kids sort of know those are things you don't do," he said. "I think our kids are pretty good that way. I'm not saying they don't go out and have a beer once in awhile, or they don't sneak a cigarette once in awhile. I'm sure some of them do. But I think most of the kids know what's at stake. When I talk to the kids at the beginning of the year, I tell them it's their football team, and for all the years before, kids have built this up to what it is, and they sacrificed, dedicated themselves, and really gave a lot to it, and now it's their turn to carry on. I tell them: 'When you're out on that field, you want to be impressive performance-wise, but you also want to be impressive gentleman-wise. And you want to be the same way off the field. You can hurt the team not only by your actions on the field, but also off the field.' "

The strict discipline of the football team is fortified by an even tougher code of conduct applied to all Moeller students. Rugged Bob Crable, as fine a linebacker as Moeller will ever have, learned that the hard way. Crable started on the Moeller varsity as a sophomore, became a prep All-American, and captained Gerry's first team at Notre Dame. A classmate who envied Bob Crable's greatness goaded him daily until a shouting and shoving match erupted in the hall. Crable was punished, and it caused him to miss a day of practice. The full wrath of Gerry Faust descended on Bob Crable and remains with him.

"I can still see him coming into the locker room," Crable said four years later. "I knew I was in trouble. He took me into the coaches' dressing room and stood me up against the door. 'What are you trying to do to this school!' he said. He was shouting. 'You're a leader; you're a captain!' He just kept shouting at me."

Once the coach had Crable's undivided attention, he calmed down enough to deliver a stern explanation of the price of greatness. It went like this:

"Listen, you're different than anybody else. You're getting recognition; you're a great athlete. God's blessed you and there are responsibilities that come with that. It's great to have all of the press and all of the glory; everybody knows Bob Crable. But Bob Crable in return has to do some things that normal kids don't have to do. You've got to learn to control yourself. You can't go in this place or that place, because you are someone who stands out in society. Whether you want to or not, you've got to set an example with self-control. Even though you may not want to do this, you have to do it, because that's part of your responsibility as a great athlete."

Gerry and Crable are very close, and they laugh about the

incident now. But both know it was no laughing matter. "His words did more to me than any physical abuse could have," Crable says. "He opened my eyes. He tried to relate everything to the real world, and everything he said was right. All of a sudden I didn't feel so indispensable." Gerry, in fact, was prepared to drop Crable permanently from the team. "He said he was sorry and it wouldn't happen again," Gerry says. "I told him, 'If it happens again, you're finished. I don't care how good you are, you're finished. You're not going to play any more, and that's it.' He knew I meant it. It killed me, but I would have done it, because you've got to set the example off the field as well as on the field."

Gerry's one great disappointment in his 21 years at Moeller involved a marginal player he cut from the team, but reinstated when he suspected the boy was a drug user. "I felt sorry for the kid, because he never was successful in life—nothing. I thought, well, the kid has never been successful at anything, and here we just dealt him another blow." The boy played very little, but his spirits and attitude seemed to improve during the football season. Never, though, could Gerry bring himself to confront the troubled young man with his suspicions of drug dependency.

"Usually when a kid's like that, they'll deny that," he said. "It's a very touchy thing to talk to a kid on something like that if you're not sure." After the season, Gerry could sense changes in the boy—a relapse. About three years after he graduated, the young man died of an overdose. To this day Gerry's most emotional feelings are directed toward the despicable agents who damage the minds and poison the bloodstreams of America's youth. "I wish that our country would have either a death penalty for sellers and pushers, or life imprisonment," he says, "because they're destroying—actually destroying—people."

Living with the Men of Moeller for 21 years, he could hardly have realized the full extent of that destruction.

THE END OF AN ERA

THE STATE FINALS: MOELLER vs. MASSILLON

November 23, 1980

The Massillon Tiger press book, which was even bigger than Moeller's media guide, established the mighty Tiger legend on the cover:
—Twenty-two times Ohio scholastic champions.
—Seven times national scholastic champions.
—Twenty undefeated seasons.
—Total attendance since 1932: 5,759,578.
—Team Record (1894 through 1979): Won 554, Lost 142, Tied 34, Winning Percentage .795.
—Average Points Per Game: Massillon 24.6, Opponents 6.8
"The Best Known Name In Scholastic Football" was the coaching home of Paul Brown for nine years; between 1932 and 1940 he compiled a winning percentage of .909, five-hundredths of a point better than Gerry Faust in his first 17 varsity seasons at Moeller. Brown left Massillon to become head coach at Ohio State, the first of six Massillon head coaches to move directly into college-level jobs. Another was Chuck Mather who won 57 and lost 3 between 1948 and 1953 and then moved on to the University of Kansas and eventually the National Football League, just as Brown did. Earle Bruce, who succeeded Woody Hayes in 1979, coached the unbeaten Tigers in 1964–65. Harry Stuldreher, one of Notre Dame's Four Horsemen, was first a Tiger.

The city of Massillon, located just down the road from Canton in northeastern Ohio, is probably the only city in America where a grown man with a family can make a living catering to the mania of one high school's football followers. Junie Studer quit a job painting signs on the sides of trucks and buildings and opened Studer's Tiger Signs in 1970. In his shop a Tiger fan can buy a Massillon shirt or a Massillon towel or a Massillon charm bracelet or even a Massillon toilet seat. As many as 20,000 people have attended Massillon games at Paul Brown Tiger Stadium; everyone in the home crowd wearing Tiger hats from Junie's, waving Tiger pennants from Junie's, and driving cars with Tiger bumper stickers from Junie's.

The games are broadcast on the only radio station in town, WTIG, of course.

Massillon is a blue-collar town, not many silver spoons at birth but plenty of tiny white-and-orange footballs. Every baby boy born at Massillon Community Hospital wakes up with one in his hand. Given this start, sons have been known to lodge with friends or relatives when their parents moved away, just so they could fulfill their destiny as Massillon Tiger football players. Not one but three booster organizations support the football team. The Tiger Booster Club provides the football coach with whatever he needs. The Tiger Touchdown Club meets at noon every Monday of the season to share lunch, watch films of the previous weekend's game, and listen to the head coach talk about that game and the next. The Sideliners are "big brothers" for the football players; each member "adopts" a player for the season, greets him before and after every game, eats with him, and listens to him and advises him.

"The key to Massillon football is the total commitment by the people in the town," the 1980 Booster Club president, steel company executive Jim Weber, said before Massillon's game with Moeller. "They think we're weird. But the way I see it is this: There are so many towns this size that have nothing. This town at least rallies around the football team. The purpose of this town during football season is to make Massillon Number One. It's not that the football team is going to play Moeller. It's the town of Massillon that's going down to play Moeller."

At first the big game was scheduled for Welcome Stadium in Dayton, because the Ohio High School Athletic Association wanted it played on a Friday night. But Welcome Stadium seats only 12,000. This was to be the biggest high school football game in history!—in Ohio history, at least. Phone calls flooded the OHSAA office in Columbus, at one point overloading the switchboard. "Get a bigger stadium," angry fans demanded. In less than 48 hours the game was switched to Nippert Stadium in Cincinnati. It meant playing on a Sunday afternoon, but 27,000 people would be able to watch.

Moeller High was a madhouse during state championship week. Phil Hersh, a writer from the Chicago *Sun-Times,* came to town to profile Gerry. "The story will run the day he gets the Notre Dame job, if he gets it. If he doesn't, it'll never be used," he said. Gerry quickly put Phil to work, as he did with everyone within reach. Phil sold tickets and answered the unrelenting telephones. "Fourteen calls in fifteen minutes at one point!" he marveled; Phil's eyebrows were arched all week. When he returned to Chicago, his one-sentence opening paragraph read: "It can't be this crazy at Notre Dame."

Moeller sold 13,500 tickets in 12 hours, and could have sold that many more. "It's going to cost me sixteen hundred dollars for 'comps,' " Gerry said late in the week. Either Gerry had too many friends, or he was simply too generous with the free tickets. Two thousand tickets unsold in Massillon were put on sale at Moeller two days before the game. People swarmed to the school, forming a line that extended through the halls, outside and around the building. Most went home empty-handed. Riverfront Stadium, capacity 55,000, might have been a better site.

Since the game was played on a Sunday, the team attended Mass together before the pre-game ritual began. The last Sunday of the 1980 season, fittingly, was also the final Sunday of the church year.

The sense of anticipation had never been greater. Marlene Faust refused to drive to the game; she was too nervous. Pat Orloff could not sleep the night before, he woke up at 1 o'clock, tossed and turned for hours, dozed off, then woke up again at 5 o'clock. Exhausted, Steve Klonne went to sleep at 7:30 in the evening, woke up to watch the 11 o'clock news, then went right back to bed.

Gerry was trotting out some old good-luck charms, a sock with a hole in the toe, a certain pair of shorts, and the floppy hat he donned for the first time when Moeller won its first state championship in 1975. He had worn it to every title game since. John Dumbacher, the statistician, strolled in, still a little dazed. John was supposed to fly to Florida on personal business; he had scheduled the trip for Sunday afternoon because Gerry had assured him the state finals would not be played on a Sunday. When the game was switched, Gerry said, "You have to be here, John! You haven't missed a game!" John was doubtful, but Gerry persuaded an airline ticket agent to assure John a seat on a flight that night. Jeff Leibert, who had proven to be the most accurate handicapper on the coaching staff and privately was predicting a two-touchdown victory early in the week, arrived that morning and confidently whispered, "Increase my spread to three."

The last team meeting of 1980 in the Moeller locker room was an emotional scene. Gerry gave his fiery, "God won't win this game" speech in response to the Massillon blasphemy, then he read a letter of support signed by every guy in the Moeller contingent at Notre Dame. It also carried best wishes under the signature of Dan Devine.

The "burnt orange and black" fanatics from Massillon had already filled their side of Nippert Stadium when Moeller arrived. It was still more than an hour before kickoff, and Moeller fans were outnumbered two-to-one. Massillon fans were chanting, "We Want Moeller! We Want Moeller!" as the Moeller players marched single file down their sideline and stopped in front of the Moeller bench. Orange and black signs in the Tiger crowd read, "Hail Mary Full of Grace, We Pray Moeller's In Second Place." The din from the wall of orange across the field would not subside. Gerry excitedly trotted the length of the field waving one raised finger in a "We're No. 1" gesture to the Moeller cheering section.

"Play it cool, guys," he said. "Just play it cool." The team nodded, the way paratroopers do before a jump. A film crew from CBS got it all for a halftime show of an NFL game to be televised on Thanksgiving Day.

In the bowels of Nippert Stadium, as the clock ticked toward kickoff, Gerry called his seniors into a separate room and closed the door. "I thought he was going to tell us this was his last game at Moeller," halfback Tim King said. He didn't. Instead he shared some very private feelings and told them they won not because of ability but because they were so close. "I love you," he said, and when the door opened he wrapped his arms around each expanse of shoulder pads as the boys left, one by one. His eyes were watery and he was sniffing as he headed down the steps toward the field, ostensibly to check on the size of the Moeller crowd.

"The Moeller fans are rising to the occasion, too," he announced when he returned. He counted off the 60 boys who would be allowed on the sideline but came up with 62. He was flipping a coin to see which two boys would spend the championship game in the stands as OHSAA commissioner Armstrong, appropriately, walked into the locker room to wish the team well.

"No antics in the end zone when we score," Gerry ordered. "We're not hot dogs and I don't want it. Any guy who does that won't get his state championship ring or watch at awards night;

that's how serious I am about this. If you want to dance around in the end zone after the game, that's fine with me. But you have to win it first." He paused to let the message sink in. "We want good, hard, clean, tough, Moeller football. Quarterbacks! Bark out your signals! Flankers! Watch the ball if you can't hear!" He paused again. "Men, this is the game we've waited seventeen years to play. None of you will ever forget this day."

Mighty Massillon was no match for mightier Moeller. With 5 minutes 24 seconds left in the first quarter, Mark Brooks bull-dozed the last three yards of a 61-yard march to make it 7–0. The first quarter was more than half over and the Massillon offense had not yet touched the ball. Rob Brown intercepted a pass on the Tigers' first play, and two plays later Brooks slammed home again. The Moeller side began to shout, "You've Got Moeller! You've Got Moeller!" The score had increased by another seven points when Gerry sent Tony Melink into the game in the last five seconds of the first half. The only thing Tony needed to become a great kicker, Gerry had said all year, was more self-confidence. This was to be a 50-yard confidence builder.

"You can make it," Gerry said, slapping Tony's backside. "You've got the wind at your back."

If there was a breeze on the field at that moment, not even the flags had noticed. Through absolutely still air, Tony Melink boomed a high kick, end over end, strong and true. He jumped two feet off the ground and trotted to the dressing room with an inconceivable three-point contribution to the Moeller lead, which stood at an insurmountable 24–0.

Gerry cleared the bench and then cleared the stands in the fourth quarter with Moeller ahead 30–0. The shutout was lost with 20 seconds to play when Moeller's second-string defense gave up a 23-yard touchdown pass. In a way, the TD and what followed made the perfect ending to a high school game. Truit Graue, a Moeller senior who played only the last few downs and was in the game for Massillon's only moment of success, stood next to Mike Cameron, his defensive backfield coach, as Massillon lined up to kick off.

"Thanks, coach, for putting me in."

"You deserved it," Cameron said reassuringly.

"It meant a lot to me, coach. It really meant a lot to me."

Gerry watched his players celebrate from the steps leading to the locker room. Some of the boys were doing belly flops in the end zone; others had formed a circle at midfield and were wiggling their hips and waving their arms. "Look at them! They're really having a ball!" He was beaming.

"You know," he said, "that's the most fun I've ever had in coaching. That scene before the game was absolutely electrifying. What a game!"

He was a man at peace, ready for a new challenge if it came.

Epilogue

A bulletin from the Associated Press cleared the sports wire in Cincinnati at 18 minutes after 4 on Monday, November 24.

> SOUTH BEND, Ind. (AP)—Gerry Faust of Moeller High School in Cincinnati Monday was named head football coach at Notre Dame, replacing Dan Devine . . . The selection of Faust, who becomes Notre Dame's 24th coach, was announced by Rev. Theodore Hesburgh . . .

The telephone call from South Bend came shortly before 3 o'clock. Gerry's first reaction was uncertainty. He went straight to Father Krusling and asked his trusted friend and boss what he should do.

"Gerry, you're ready for it," Father said. "I can't picture you sitting in front of a television set next October, watching Notre Dame and knowing you could have been the coach, and being anything but unhappy with yourself for passing up an opportunity like that. It's something you've always wanted. You have to do it."

That was all Gerry needed. He and Marlene hit the road, out of the reach of every telephone, microphone, and television camera in America until the next morning in South Bend.

The news came as no surprise to anyone, but the reality of it was a shock to many. No longer would his frenetic figure prowl the Moeller halls or his scratchy voice pierce the air and grate against the tiled walls. The young men he left behind remembered him in touching, personal ways and talked as though he had been taken up to heaven. Junior quarterback Mike Willging told how Gerry helped him and his family cope with the death of his brother in an auto accident three years earlier; defensive end Chuck Lima recalled how Gerry changed his mind when he was thinking of skipping football to play in a band; Kentuckian Ron Davis relived his first day at Moeller when Gerry personally showed him around the school. "I've never gone to Moeller without him being in the building somewhere," he said.

"I'm sure when I sit down to do my homework tonight I'll be thinking of him," said linebacker Mike Harmeyer. "We won't be playing under him," said Rob Brown, "but we'll feel his presence."

Three men were named to replace Gerry. Solid Ted Bacigalupo accepted the job of head football coach, with an understandably dry mouth, and promised to do his best, which is all anyone could ask or hope to deliver in such a situation. Steady Mike Cameron became athletic director, guaranteeing an orderly transition and, overall, better organization. Jeff Leibert, personable and a hustler, assumed Gerry's fund-raising and program responsibilities. Coach Baci was left with a better than usual nucleus, 11 experienced players, and a tougher than usual schedule—the highlight a regular-season rematch with Massillon at Paul Brown Tiger Stadium. The biggest holes he had to fill were not in the lineup but on the staff. He needed an offensive line coach to replace Jim Higgins, who went to Notre Dame with Gerry, and a linebacker coach and defensive coordinator to replace himself. He planned to run the offense, just as Gerry had.

For the first year at least, keeping it going without Gerry seemed to be a mission that would sustain everyone, coaches and players alike. Only time would tell. The Pack never really came back after Lombardi left, and UCLA's exclusive claim to the national championship in college basketball ended abruptly with John Wooden's retirement. History seemed to say some kind of decline in Moeller's dominance was inevitable with the departure of its coaching legend. Within the school itself Gerry's exit meant several people who had labored so long in his shadow would at last have an opportunity to grow and excel as administrators and leaders. The vacuum would be large but not infinite.

By virtually any yardstick, the 1980 season was both Gerry's and Moeller's finest. Nearly 167,000 people watched the 13 games Moeller played. Excluding their losses to Moeller, the 12 regular-season and playoff opponents had a combined record of 90 victories, 22 defeats, and 2 ties—a winning percentage only slightly lower than Moeller's own for 17 seasons. The 1980 Moeller team was not blessed with an abundance of gifted athletes. In truth, the squad was closer to an average high school team than any Moeller state champion since the first one. This Moeller team could easily have lost at least four games. Coaching, tradition, and hard work prevailed.

The most appropriate postscript to Gerry's final season at Moeller came immediately after his last game. He insisted that the state championship trophy be presented to his dad, "because he's the best coach who ever lived" and "because he went up there in 1946 and Massillon beat Chaminade real bad (35–12)." Fuzzy Faust accepted the trophy and said to his son's last team:

"You were the poorest Moeller team in the last ten years starting out. But you made more improvement than any Moeller team in history. You worked hard and you worked together. You showed what hard work can do. You played the toughest schedule we've ever had; you beat some outstanding teams. You've earned this championship and you should be proud of it."